Jack C. Richards & Chuck Sandy

Passages

Second Edition

Student's Book 2

CAMBRIDGE
UNIVERSITY PRESS

Jo Ann Johnson

CAMBRIDGE UNIVERSITY PRESS
Cambridge, New York, Melbourne, Madrid, Cape Town,
Singapore, São Paulo, Delhi, Mexico City

Cambridge University Press
32 Avenue of the Americas, New York, NY10013-2473, USA

www.cambridge.org
Information on this title: www.cambridge.org/9780521683913

First published 1998
Second Edition 2008
15th printing 2013

Printed in Hong Kong, China, by Golden Cup Printing Company Limited

A catalog record for this publication is available from the British Library.

Library of Congress Cataloging-in-Publication Data

Richards, Jack C.
Passages: student's book 2 / by Jack C. Richards & Chuck Sandy. – 2nd ed.
   p. cm.
ISBN 978-0-521-68388-3 (pbk. with audio cd/cd-rom)
1. English language – Textbooks for foreign speakers. 2. English language – Problems, exercises, etc. I. Sandy, Chuck. II. Title.

PE1128.R4599 2008
428.2'4–dc22

2007045432

ISBN 978-0-521-68391-3student's book with self-study audio CD/CD-ROM (Windows, Mac)
ISBN 978-0-521-68393-7workbook
ISBN 978-0-521-68392-0 teacher's edition and audio CD
ISBN 978-0-521-68395-1 CDs (audio)

Art direction, book design, photo research, and layout services: Adventure House, NYC
Audio production: Paul Ruben Productions

Authors' Acknowledgments

A great number of people contributed to the development of *Passages, Second Edition*. Particular thanks are owed to the following:

The **reviewers** using *Passages* in the following schools and institutes – their insights and suggestions have helped define the content and format of the second edition: Maria Elizabeth Andrews from **Proficiency School of English**, São Paulo, Brazil; Vera Lúcia Cardoso Berk from **Talkative Idioms Center**, São Paulo, Brazil; coordinators and teachers from **Phil Young's English School**, Curitiba, Brazil; Janette Carvalhinho de Oliveira, Manoel Sampaio Junior, and Sandlei Moraes de Oliveira from **Centro de Línguas para a Comunidade,** Vitória, Brazil; Juliana Costa da Silva, Soraya Farage Martins, Valdemir Pinto da Silva Jr., and Luciana Ribeiro da Silva from **Alternative Language Learning**, Rio de Janeiro, Brazil; Danielle Sampaio Cordeiro from **Sociedade Brasileira de Cultura Inglesa**, Rio de Janeiro, Brazil; Inara Lúcia Castillo Couto from **CEL-LEP**, São Paulo, Brazil; Mailda Flôres Sales, Maria Helena Medrado, and Sávio Siqueira from **ACBEU**, Salvador, Brazil; Angela Graciela Mendonza dos Santos from **Focus Consultoria Educacional**, Rio de Janeiro, Brazil; Caroline Ciagiwoda and Aguirre Pinto Neto from **Exien English School**, Curitiba, Brazil; Evânia A. Netto and Anderson Lopes Siqueira from **ICBEU**, São José dos Campos, Brazil; Silvia Sapiense from **Speed English Center**, São Paulo, Brazil; Michael Twohey from **York University**, Toronto, Canada; Randa Ibrahim Mady and Magda Laurence from the **Centre for Adult and Continuing Education, the American University of Cairo**, Cairo, Egypt; Jamie Dupuis, Dale Palmer, Kent Suder, and Stephanie Wilson from **GEOS**, Japan; Gregory Hadley from **Niigata University of International and Information Studies**, Niigata, Japan; Brian Quinn from **Kyushu University**, Fukuoka, Japan; David Michael Duke, Christine A. Figueroa, and Thomas Greene from **Kyung Hee University**, Seoul, Korea; Jinyoung Hong, Susan Kelly, Young-Ok Kim, Jennifer Lee, and Scott Miles from **Sogang University**, Seoul, Korea; Christopher N. Payne from **Seoul National University, Language Education Institute**, Seoul, Korea; Julia Samuel from **Sahmyook University English Department**, Seoul, Korea; Juan Alvarez Cháves from **Instituto Technologico Superior de Zapotlanejo**, Jalisco, Mexico; Samuel Bolaños Whangpo, Luis G. Dominguez Arellano, and Diana Jones from **Centro Universitario Angloamericano**, Mexico City, Mexico; A. Ezequiel Guerrero Marín and Lino Martín Lugo Córdova from **Centro de Estudio de Idiomas-UAS**, Los Mochis, Mexico; Olga Hernández Badillo, Leticia Moreno Elizalde, and Fernando Perales Vargas from **Facultad de Contaduría y Administración de la Universidad Juarez del Estado de Durango**, Durango, Mexico; Yuriria Tabakova Hernández from **Universidad Latinoamericana**, Mexico City, Mexico; Lucila Mendoza Reyes from **Universidad Autonoma Metropolitana**, Mexico City, Mexico; Roberto López Rodríguez from **Centro de Auto-Aprendizaje de Inglés, Facultad de Ciencias Físico Matemáticas UANL**, San Nicolas de los Garza, Mexico; Elizabeth Almandoz, Susanna D. de Eguren, and Rocío García Valdez from **Instituto Cultural Peruano Norteamericano (ICPNA)**, Miraflores, Peru; Giuliana B. Astorne Guillén from **CED El Buen Pastor**, Lima, Peru; Cecilia Carmelino from **ICPNA**, La Molina, Peru; César Ccaccya Leiva from **ICPNA**, San Miguel, Peru; Amparo García Peña from **ICPNA**, Cusco, Peru; Elizabeth Llatas Castillo from **Centro Binacional El Cultural**, Trujillo, Peru; Claudia Marín Cabrera from **Universidad Peruana de Ciencias Aplicadas**, Lima, Peru; Silvia Osores and María Isabel Valencia from **Colegio de La Immaculada**, Lima, Peru; Samuel Chen from **Taichung YMCA Language School**, Taichung, Taiwan; Shih-Wen Chen from **National Tsing Hua University Department of Foreign Languages and Literature**, Hsinchu, Taiwan; Han-yi Lin from **Center of Foreign Languages, National Chengchi University**, Taipei, Taiwan; Huei-chih Liu from **Shu-Te University**, Kaohsiung, Taiwan; Julie D. Adler, Beth Kozbial Ernst, and Kelly Wonder from **University of Wisconsin-Eau Claire**, Eau Claire, Wisconsin, USA; Renata Concina, Mary Horosco, Margaret A. Lowry, and Luis Sanchez from **The English Language Institute at Florida International University**, Miami, Florida, USA; Mary Gillman from **Des Moines Area Community College**, Des Moines, Iowa, USA; Leslie Lott from **Embassy CES**, Fort Lauderdale, Florida, USA; Paul Paitchell from **Talk International**, Fort Lauderdale, Florida, USA; Elisa Shore from **City College of San Francisco**, San Francisco, California, USA; Theresa E. Villa from **East Los Angeles Skills Center**, Los Angeles, California, USA; Randi Wilder, Upper Saddle River, New Jersey, USA.

The **editorial** and **production** team: Sue Brioux Aldcorn, Sue Andre Costello, Eleanor K. Barnes, David Bohlke, Mike Boyle, Jeff Chen, Sarah Cole, Inara Lucia Castillo Couto, Leslie DeJesus, Jill Freshney, Rod Gammon, Deborah Goldblatt, Paul Heacock, Louisa Hellegers, Lisa Hutchins, Genevieve Kocienda, Cindy Leaney, Linda LiDestri, Andy London, Paul MacIntyre, Diana Nam, Margareth Perucci, Sandra Pike, Mary Sandre, Tamar Savir, Satoko Shimoyama, Susannah Sodergren, Lori Solbakken, Louisa van Houten, Mary Vaughn, Jennifer Wilkin, Jenny Wilsen, and all the design and production team at Adventure House.

And Cambridge University Press **staff** and **advisors**: Sarah Acosta, Harry Ahn, Yumiko Akeba, Jim Anderson, Mary Louise Baez, Kathleen Corley, Kate Cory-Wright, Maiza Fatureto, Claudia Fiocco, Elizabeth Fuzikava, Cecilia Gómez, Heather Gray, Yuri Hara, Catherine Higham, Peter Holly, Jennifer Kim, Robert Kim, Ken Kingery, Kareen Kjelstrup, Gareth Knight, Nigel McQuitty, João Madureira, Andy Martin, Alejandro Martínez, John Moorcroft, Mark O'Neil, Marcus Paiva, Orelly Palmas, Jinhee Park, Walter Quiroz, Carlos Ramírez, Ricardo Romero, Tereza Sekiya, Catherine Shih, Howard Siegelman, Ivan Sorrentino, Ian Sutherland, Alcione Soares Tavares, Koen Van Landeghem, Sergio Varela, and Ellen Zlotnick.

Additional thanks are owed to Cindy Leaney for writing the Self-study section and to Sue Brioux Aldcorn for writing the Grammar Plus section.

Welcome to Passages!

Passages, Second Edition, is a two-level course that will help you raise your English to the next level. You've already learned the basics and have progressed to the advanced level. To take you further, *Passages, Second Edition*, emphasizes new and sophisticated grammar and vocabulary, listening and reading texts on more challenging topics, academic writing activities, and thought-provoking discussions.

There is a Self-study section to help build your academic skills, and this book also includes the *Cambridge Academic Content Dictionary* on CD-ROM.

Each unit consists of two four-page lessons. Each lesson contains a variety of exercises, including starting point, vocabulary, grammar, listening, discussion, writing, and reading. Here is a sample unit.

Unit features

Starting point presents new grammar in both formal and conversational contexts.

Vocabulary teaches phrasal verbs, prefixes and suffixes, and collocations (words that go together).

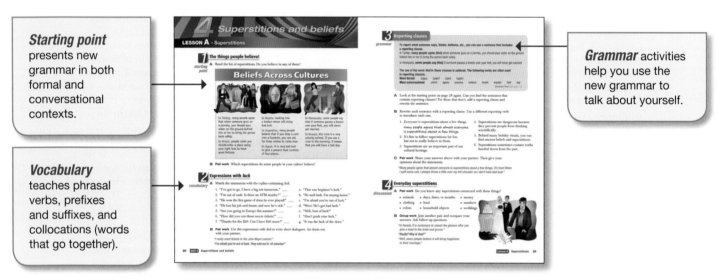

Grammar activities help you use the new grammar to talk about yourself.

Listening activities develop skills such as listening for main ideas, making inferences, and note taking.

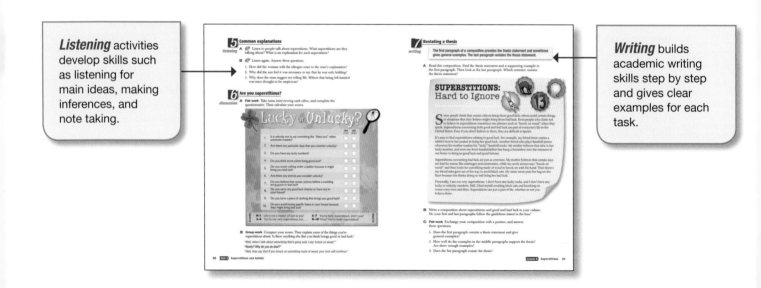

Writing builds academic writing skills step by step and gives clear examples for each task.

Lesson B is a complete four-page lesson, with new grammar and vocabulary, and a new twist on the unit topic.

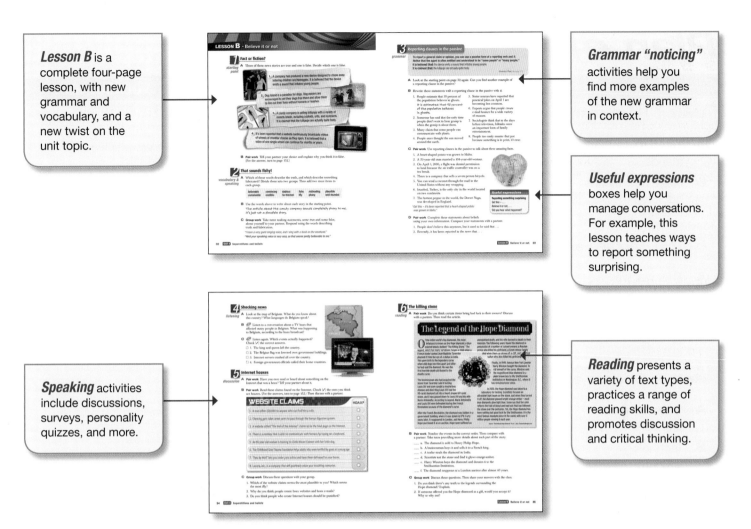

Grammar "noticing" activities help you find more examples of the new grammar in context.

Useful expressions boxes help you manage conversations. For example, this lesson teaches ways to report something surprising.

Speaking activities include discussions, surveys, personality quizzes, and more.

Reading presents a variety of text types, practices a range of reading skills, and promotes discussion and critical thinking.

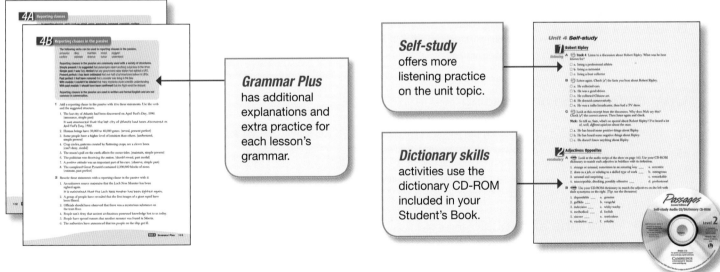

Grammar Plus has additional explanations and extra practice for each lesson's grammar.

Self-study offers more listening practice on the unit topic.

Dictionary skills activities use the dictionary CD-ROM included in your Student's Book.

More resources

Communication reviews after every three units include progress checks and additional listening and speaking activities.

The **Workbook** gives you language practice and extra reading and writing activities.

The **Teacher's Edition** includes additional games, projects, and readings, as well as written and oral quizzes.

Plan of Book 2

	FUNCTIONS	GRAMMAR	VOCABULARY
Unit 1 Relationships pages 2–9			
A The best of friends **B** Make new friends, but keep the old . . .	• Defining and describing friendship • Expressing opinions • Stating preferences • Sharing friendship advice	• Phrasal verbs • Gerund and infinitive constructions	• Adjectives to describe friendship • *re-* words
Unit 2 Clothes and appearance pages 10–17			
A The way we dress **B** How we appear to others	• Discussing approaches to fashion • Describing style and trends • Expressing opinions about clothing • Talking about first impressions • Describing appearances	• Review of verb patterns • Cleft sentences with *what*	• Adjectives describing style • Adjectives describing outward appearance
Unit 3 Science and technology pages 18–25			
A Good science, bad science **B** Technology and you	• Talking about scientific advances • Analyzing the effects of science and technology • Describing technology troubles	• Indefinite and definite articles • *-ing* clauses	• Adjectives used to discuss issues associated with technology • Collocations used to express different attitudes
Units 1-3 Communication review pages 26–27			
Unit 4 Superstitions and beliefs pages 28–35			
A Superstitions **B** Believe it or not	• Talking about personal beliefs • Comparing beliefs • Reporting what someone else believes • Expressing opinions	• Reporting clauses • Reporting clauses in the passive	• Expressions with *luck* • Adjectives to describe truth and fabrication
Unit 5 Television and reading pages 36–43			
A Television **B** Trends in reading	• Discussing your favorite TV programs • Discussing advantages and disadvantages of TV • Talking about the role of reading in your life • Discussing trends in reading and technology	• *Such . . . that* and *so . . . that* • Sentence adverbs	• Nouns for types of TV programs • Adjectives to describe reading material
Unit 6 Musicians and music pages 44–51			
A A world of music **B** Getting your big break	• Reading and sharing views on music • Expressing preferences • Comparing and contrasting • Defining success • Commenting on facts	• Double comparatives • *Will* and *would* for habits and general truths	• Collocations used to describe music • Idioms used in the entertainment industry
Units 4-6 Communication review pages 52–53			

SPEAKING	LISTENING	WRITING	READING
• Talking about what friends should have in common • Talking about the best way to meet friends • Discussing ways to maintain relationships	• A talk about differences between friendships among men and friendships among women • A young woman describes a chance encounter	• Developing a thesis statement • Writing paragraphs supporting a thesis statement	• "The Value of Cyber-Friendship": How the Internet is changing friendships
• Discussing different opinions on fashion • Discussing how first impressions are formed • Discussing tips for making a good first impression • Discussing how people respond to appearance	• Three people describe their approach to clothes • Three people explain how first impressions affect them	• Writing a composition about a personal belief • Giving examples to support a thesis statement	• "First Impressions Count": How to make a good first impression
• Discussing the positive effects and negative consequences of technology and science • Discussing your feelings about new technology • Taking a survey about your relationship with technology	• A reporter discusses genetically modified food • A comedian talks about difficulties he has with technology in his house	• Writing summaries • Writing a summary of a short article • Identifying essential information	• "Who Are the Amish?": A different approach to technology
• Describing superstitions from your country or culture • Discussing different views on superstitions • Taking a survey of beliefs • Telling stories • Discussing hoaxes and why people create them	• A number of people give explanations for superstitions • Two people discuss a TV hoax	• Restating the thesis in the last paragraph • Giving general examples • Writing a composition about superstitions	• "The Legend of the Hope Diamond": The history of "The Killing Stone"
• Discussing the positive and negative influences of TV • Talking about results of a reading survey	• TV critics discuss popular TV shows • Two people talk about how people benefit from reading literature	• Writing a review of a TV program • Including essential information in a review	• "Reviews from Readers": Book reviews
• Talking about personal tastes • Talking about styles of music • Discussing the role of music in different contexts • Choosing the best advice for success	• Two people share their opinions on different songs • A young woman gives her friend advice on his music career	• Writing a compare-and-contrast essay • Describing similarities and differences	• "Making Music Under the Streets of New York": Subway musicians

SPEAKING	LISTENING	WRITING	READING
• Discussing lifestyle trends • Talking about the results of a survey on how well you cope with change	• Two young people discuss the differences between their generation and that of their parents' • Two people discuss how to preserve photos and film	• Writing about a personal experience • Writing about past events • Providing details	• "Leaving the Rat Race for the Simple Life": Reflections on a major change in lifestyle
• Discussing compulsive shopping • Talking about the best ways to shop for different items • Discussing advertising campaigns and undercover marketing strategies	• Two people talk about shopping preferences • Three radio advertisements	• Supporting an opinion • Writing a composition about shopping	• "Guerrillas in Our Midst": Marketing gimmicks
• Discussing the ethics of using animals in different fields • Discussing a survey on ethics associated with animals • Talking about the convenience or inconvenience of owning a pet	• Reports on unusual ways in which animals help people • A pet shop owner talks about suitable pets	• Writing a classification essay • Organizing information into clear categories	• "Kennel of the Mind": Do some pets benefit from a psychologist?
• Discussing a survey on public speaking • Giving advice on how to tell interesting stories • Discussing problems with language • Talking about "text speak" and its appropriateness	• An expert gives advice on how to make effective presentations • Three one-sided conversations	• Persuasive writing • Supporting a position • Arguing against the opposing position	• "Slang Abroad": Different varieties of English
• Discussing people who have made an impact in your country • Discussing the qualities and guiding principles of exceptional people • Discussing famous quotations • Talking about heroic behavior in our everyday lives	• A motivational speaker talks about the qualities of high achievers • Two people talk about others who have made a difference in their lives	• Writing a biography • Organizing paragraphs in chronological order • Using time words and phrases in a composition	• "Ann Cotton, Social Entrepreneur": Volunteering is an opportunity to help people
• Discussing job advertisements • Discussing a survey on work environments and your ideal job • Analyzing the qualities of the ideal job • Discussing the qualities of a successful worker	• Two people discuss unsuccessful business ventures • Three people talk about workshops they attended	• Writing formal letters • Understanding the parts of a formal letter	• "The Value of Difference": Individual differences in the workplace

Relationships

1 The nature of friendship

starting point

A Read these statements about friendship. Can you explain what they mean? What other statements would you add to the list?

What is a friend?

1. A friend is someone who brings out the best in you.
2. Good friends are always happy to help when you run into a problem.
3. A friend is someone who cheers you up when you're feeling bad.
4. True friends don't drift apart even after many years of separation.
5. A real friend will always stand up for you when others are putting you down.
6. Never be afraid to open up and ask a friend for advice. A true friend will never turn you down.
7. Make new friends, but hang on to the old ones.
8. Good friends are hard to come by, harder to leave, and impossible to do without.

"The first statement means a good friend will reveal all your positive qualities."

B **Group work** Consider the statements above. What makes a good friend? Discuss with your group.

"In my opinion, a good friend is someone who makes you a better person. It's someone who brings out the best in you."

> **Useful expressions**
>
> **Expressing opinions**
> In my opinion, . . .
> I have to say that . . .
> The way I see it, . . .
> Personally, I (don't) think . . .

2 Friendship among women and men

listening & speaking

A Listen to a professor talk about author Deborah Tannen's ideas. In Tannen's opinion, what is the main difference between friendship among men and friendship among women?

B Listen again. According to Tannen, which of these things do male friends do (*M*) and which do female friends do (*F*)? Write the correct letter.

____ 1. looks for a point   ____ 4. give and get facts

____ 2. discuss a topic in detail   ____ 5. do things together

____ 3. share feelings and secrets   ____ 6. have long conversations

C **Group work** Do you agree or disagree with Tannen's ideas about friendship? Why or why not?

"I have to say that I think some of her ideas are really accurate . . ."

3 Phrasal verbs

grammar

A phrasal verb is a verb plus a particle, such as *down*, *into*, *out*, or *up*.
The meaning of a phrasal verb is different from the meaning of its parts.

Separable phrasal verbs can take objects before or after the particle.
If the object is a pronoun, it always appears before the particle.
A friend is someone who **brings out** the best in you.
A friend is someone who **brings** the best **out** in you.
A friend is someone who **cheers** you **up** when you're feeling bad.

With inseparable phrasal verbs, the object cannot go between the verb and the particle.
Good friends are always happy to help when you **run into** a problem.

Three-word phrasal verbs have a particle and a preposition.
Make new friends, but **hang on to** the old ones.

Intransitive phrasal verbs don't take objects.
True friends don't **drift apart**.

Grammar Plus: See page 106.

A Look at the starting point on page 2 again. Can you find more phrasal verbs? Which are separable, inseparable, and/or three-word verbs? Which are also intransitive? Write them in the chart.

Separable	Inseparable	Three-word verbs	Intransitive

B Complete the questions below with the phrasal verbs and objects in parentheses. Sometimes more than one answer is possible.

1. Have you ever had a friend who <u>brought out the worst /</u> <u>brought the worst out</u> (bring out / the worst) in you?

2. Have you ever _____ (run into / a friend) that you hadn't seen in a long time?

3. Do you usually _____ (stand up for / your friends) when other people criticize them?

4. Can you _____ (do without / a cell phone) and still keep in touch with friends?

5. When friends ask you for a favor, do you usually say yes, or do you _____ (turn down / them)?

6. Do you _____ (hang on to / your old friends), or do you drift apart as time goes by?

7. Some people like to _____ (put down / their friends) by insulting them. How would you feel if a friend did that to you?

C **Pair work** Discuss the questions above.

"Have you ever had a friend who brought out the worst in you?"

"Yeah, I once had a really messy roommate. She made me so angry."

4 Describing friendship

vocabulary

A **Pair work** Complete the chart with the correct parts of speech.

	Verb	Adjective		Verb	Adjective
1.	admire		4.	empathize	
2.		beneficial	5.	endure	
3.	clash		6.		harmonious

B Choose the word from the chart above that best replaces the boldfaced words. Compare answers with a partner.

1. Ryan and Tina work to keep their friendship **free of conflict**. *harmonious*
2. Sometimes their opinions **are very different**, but they still get along.
3. They work to make their friendship **valuable and constructive**.
4. Having the same background helps them **understand and identify** with each other.
5. Ryan and Tina **think very highly of** each other's accomplishments.
6. Their friendship will certainly **last a long time**.

5 What should friends have in common?

discussion

A Look at the statements about friendship in the chart. Do you agree with the statements? Add a statement of your own.

People . . .	Agree	Disagree
1. who are close in age empathize with each other better.	☐	☐
2. with similar social backgrounds have more harmonious friendships.	☐	☐
3. who have similar values and beliefs have stronger connections.	☐	☐
4. with similar personalities have the most enduring friendships.	☐	☐
5. benefit from having friends with the same educational background.	☐	☐
6. should only mingle with friends who have the same interests.	☐	☐
7. from different cultures often clash with each other.	☐	☐
8. _____	☐	☐

B **Group work** Share your opinions, and explain your reasons.

"The way I see it, people who are close in age can empathize better with each other. They share the same experiences and understand each other."

"I see your point, but I think age isn't that important. If people like doing similar things, they can be good friends."

C **Group work** How many people agreed or disagreed with each statement? Report your findings to the class.

"Three of us agreed that friends who are close in age relate better . . ."

Useful expressions

Disagreeing politely
I see your point, but . . .
I see what you mean, but . . .
I'm not sure I agree.
Do you think so?

Developing a thesis statement

The first paragraph of a composition contains a thesis statement, which presents the main idea. The remaining paragraphs each have a single focus expressed in a topic sentence that develops the thesis statement.

A Read the composition. Underline the thesis statement in the first paragraph.

B Match each of the other paragraphs with the phrase below that best summarizes its focus.

___ why we have a   ___ what we have   ___ how we
    close friendship   in common   are different

1 My best friend Eva and I are different in many ways, but we have one important thing in common – we love to travel. Whenever I have the urge to explore a new place, I can always count on Eva to go with me. Our friendship shows that people who are very different can still have similar interests.

2 The differences between Eva and me are significant. Eva is an artist who loves to take photographs and draw pictures of the interesting things she sees. I am a sales representative for a pharmaceutical company and spend most of my time calculating numbers. Eva is a very impulsive person, but I'm very organized. She's very quiet, but I'm a very talkative person who enjoys telling stories.

3 Eva and I are both adventurous and love traveling. We discovered this shortly after we met several years ago. One day we were talking about vacations, and we found we had both visited many of the same places. We immediately made a plan to go to a nearby historical city the following weekend.

4 Although we are quite different in many ways, Eva and I have become close over the years, and we now have a very special and enduring friendship. Every time we get together, we always have so much to talk about and have the best time. One reason for this is that we share a love of travel and adventure. The other reason is that our differences complement each other, so we always get along well whenever we travel together.

C Write a composition about a close friend. Then exchange your composition with a partner, and answer these questions.

1. What is the thesis statement? Underline it.

2. Does each paragraph have a single focus? Write the focus for each in the margin of the paper.

3. What else would you like to know about your partner's friend? Ask at least two questions.

Meeting new people

starting point

A Read about how Yuan-lin, Jacob, and Jackie met new people. Which way of meeting people do you like the best?

Yuan-lin
"I decided to move to England last year. I felt really lonely at first. In fact, I regretted moving here. But I never gave up trying new things. Then, I saw an ad for a Chinese-English language exchange. It was a great way to meet cool people!"

Jackie
"I'd been planning to take a class, but was putting off enrolling. Well, last month I started taking a history class. I never expected to meet so many people! A few classmates formed a study group, and we've become really good friends."

Jacob
"I didn't know many people at my new job, but I kept being invited by my co-workers to a lunchtime yoga class. I'm so glad I finally said yes! A couple of my colleagues play soccer too, and they're considering starting a company team!"

"A language exchange is a great idea. You can meet people who are interested in the same language and culture, so everyone already has something in common."

B Group work What other ways of meeting new people can you suggest for these situations? Add another situation to the list.

someone who . . .

- moved to a new neighborhood
- has little free time
- started a new job
- is very shy
- is over 65 years old
- _____

A chance meeting

listening

A Pair work When was the last time you unexpectedly ran into someone you know? Tell your partner about your experience.

B Listen to Debbie talk about how she met her friend Kate. Where were they when they first met? Where were they when they met again?

C Listen again. Then answer the following questions.

1. Why were Debbie and Kate going to Los Angeles?
2. What did Debbie regret after she said goodbye to Kate?
3. How much time passed between their first and second meetings?
4. How did Samantha, the guest at the party, know Kate?

3 Gerund and infinitive constructions

grammar

These verbs are normally followed by a gerund: *appreciate, consider, enjoy, give up, keep, put off, suggest.*
They're **considering starting** a company team!

These verbs are normally followed by an infinitive: *ask, decide, expect, intend, need, refuse, seem, tend.*
I never **expected to meet** so many people!

These verbs are followed by either a gerund or an infinitive: *begin, bother, continue, hate, prefer, start.*
Last month I **started taking / to take** a history class.

Infinitives and gerunds can also occur in the passive voice. They follow the pattern
subject + verb + *being / to be* + past participle.
I **kept being invited** by my co-workers to a lunchtime yoga class.
She **asked to be chosen** for the job.   *Grammar Plus: See page 107.*

A Look at the starting point again on page 6. Can you find another verb that is followed by a gerund and another verb that is followed by an infinitive?

B Circle the correct form of the verbs. Sometimes both answers are possible.

◀ ▶   C   +   🔗 http://www.cup.org/friendship   Q▾ Search

MONDAY, MARCH 18

I've never been a really popular guy. I'm the type of person who tends **1** *to have / having* one or two good friends rather than lots of acquaintances. Well, when I moved away from my hometown after getting a job in another city, I really needed **2** *to make / making* some new friends. Because I'm shy, I considered **3** *to change / changing* my personality to become more outgoing. But that was very difficult for me. Just the same, I didn't give up **4** *to try / trying*. I decided **5** *to create / creating* a new image for myself. I bought myself some new shoes, new clothes, and I even got a new haircut and started **6** *to wear / wearing* contact lenses. However, it didn't seem **7** *to change / changing* anything. I was beginning to regret **8** *to leave / leaving* my hometown when, all of a sudden, I got a call from my old friend Jim. He was planning **9** *to move / moving* here pretty soon. He wanted some advice about finding an apartment here in the city, and I suggested **10** *to share / sharing* an apartment with me. Well, he agreed! I really enjoy **11** *to have / having* someone to spend time with − together we've met some new friends.

Posted by <u>DenverDan</u>   💬   <u>2 COMMENTS</u>

C **Pair work** Complete these sentences with your own information, and add more details. Then compare with a partner.

1. I don't like it when friends refuse . . .

   to do small favors for me, like lending me a book. It's so rude.

2. It can be annoying when friends ask . . .

3. I couldn't say no if a friend suggested . . .

4. Even when they disagree, friends should continue . . .

4 re- words

vocabulary

A Which word best completes these sentences? Write the correct letter.

a. rebuild   c. reconnect   e. rehash   g. resurface
b. recall   d. redefine   f. rekindle   h. reunion

1. You can _f_ old friendships by sharing memories.

2. Don't _E_ old arguments over and over.

3. People often _D_ themselves, but they're essentially the same person.

4. Try to attend a high school or college _h_ .

5. Can you _G_ the first time you met your best friend?

6. With e-mail, people often _C_ after being out of touch for years.

7. Visit your hometown and _b_ with your roots. *Roots*

8. It takes time to _A_ a damaged friendship.

B **Pair work** What other *re-* words do you know? How would you define them? Compare your list with a partner.

Recapture, reconsider, . . .

5 Friendship maintenance

discussion

A Look at these ideas for maintaining friendships. Choose three that you think are the most important.

Advice for Maintaining FRIENDSHIPS

- Send cards on holidays or birthdays. People appreciate getting cards on special occasions.

- Never betray a trust – it can cause real resentment.

- Try to be completely honest with your friends at all times.

- Attend school reunions and other similar social events. It may give you the chance to rebuild old friendships and reminisce about good times.

- Send an occasional e-mail or photo to friends whom you haven't seen in a while.

- Be a good listener, and try to empathize with your friends.

- Respect your friends' point of view even when you disagree. Don't rehash old arguments.

- Be aware of "unhealthy" friendships. In some cases, it's better to end a friendship and move on with your life.

B **Group work** Tell your group which three pieces of advice you chose, and explain why. Then share any other ideas you have about maintaining friendships.

"Well, I think it's important to always be completely honest with your friends. If you aren't honest with your friends, they might not be honest with you."

Useful expressions

Agreeing on importance

Well, I think it's important . . .
Yeah, that's true, but even more important is . . .
And let's not forget . . .
You're right . . . is also quite important.

6. Technology and friendship

A Read the article. Then check (✓) the best subtitle.

☐ a. How our relationships are changing   ☐ b. How to make more friends online

THE VALUE OF CYBER FRIENDSHIP

CYBERSPACE HAS GIVEN WAY TO A NEW SOCIAL dynamic where people make friends from across the globe, but know little about their next-door neighbors. The abandoning of the "village mentality" disturbs critics, but those who have been won over often find an Internet friendship more satisfying. Some new research is also showing how e-mail and the Internet supplement, rather than replace, the communication people have with others in their social network.

Take Bob for example. His neighbor doesn't know anything about gardening and lawn care, but his instant messaging buddy Gr33nThum does. Besides, Gr33nThum is more interesting and doesn't do that annoying clicking sound when he talks.

This newly evolved form of hyper-connected human has long been criticized for his or her lack of necessary social skills. His preference for textual relations over face-to-face interaction has given the traditionalist fits. In short, say critics, people are unlearning how to naturally interact with their neighbors, creating a social network of strangers.

However, a report entitled "The Strength of Internet Ties" suggests a different scenario altogether. Sociologists are suggesting that the Internet helps cultivate social networks and make use of them when it matters most.

Friends often move. As kids, our friends' parents move away. As adults, we move away to college or for work. Communicative tools have made losing touch the result of sheer laziness, not distance. "The larger, the more far-flung, and the more diverse a person's network, the more important e-mail is," argues Jeffrey Boase, who co-authored the report on the strength of Internet ties. "You can't make phone calls or personal visits to all your friends very often, but you can 'cc' them regularly with a couple of keystrokes. That turns out to be very important."

In addition to expanding and strengthening the social ties people maintain in the offline world, Internet and e-mail provide a social and informational support group that helps people make difficult decisions and face challenges. The survey found that Internet users are more likely than non-users to have been helped by those in their social networks as they faced important events in their life.

"Internet use provides online [users] a path to resources, such as access to people who may have the right information to help deal with family health crises or find a new job," says John Horrigan, author of the report.

"The Internet and the cell phone have transformed communication: Instead of being based on house-to-house interactions, they are built on person-to-person exchanges," says co-author Barry Wellman. "This creates a new basis for community. Rather than relying on a single community for social support, individuals often must actively seek out a variety of appropriate people and resources for different situations."

Source: "The Value of Cyber-Friendship," by Jason Lee Miller, WebProNews

B **Group work** Discuss these questions. Then share your answers with the class.

1. How do you use the Internet to communicate? Do you have e-mail? write a blog? use instant messaging?

2. Do you spend more time communicating in person, by phone, or online? What are the advantages and disadvantages of each?

3. What predictions can you make about how technology will impact friendships?

2 Clothes and appearance

LESSON A · The way we dress

1 Fashion sense

starting point

A What's your approach to fashion? Complete this survey.

CLOTHING SURVEY

	Agree	Disagree
1. When I choose clothes, I tend to think of comfort first and appearance second.	☐	☐
2. I hate choosing my outfits in the morning. I just put on anything I can find.	☐	☐
3. Celebrities sometimes inspire me to change the way I look.	☐	☐
4. Companies should discourage employees from wearing casual clothes to work.	☐	☐
5. I don't like to draw attention to myself, so I wear pretty conventional clothes.	☐	☐
6. I enjoy shopping for clothes. I don't mind spending hours in clothing stores.	☐	☐
7. High prices rarely prevent me from buying quality clothing.	☐	☐
8. Peer pressure sometimes compels me to wear brand name clothing.	☐	☐

B Group work Discuss your answers to the survey.

"I tend to think of comfort first when I choose clothes. When I'm comfortable, I feel good, and that's more important to me than looking good."

2 Judging by appearances

discussion

A Pair work Read these famous quotations. In your own words, explain to a partner what they mean.

It's always the badly dressed people who are the most interesting.
— Jean Paul Gaultier

Eat to please oneself, but dress to please others.
– Benjamin Franklin

Three-tenths of good looks are due to nature; seven-tenths to dress.
– Chinese proverb

"I think the first one means interesting people focus more on meaningful things."

B Group work Discuss these questions.

1. Do you think it's fair for people to judge you by the way you dress?
2. Do you judge others by the way they dress?
3. Would you be friends with someone whose style was very different from your own?
4. Would you change the way you dress to please someone else?

3 Review of verb patterns

grammar

Study the following common verb patterns.

a. verb + infinitive
When I choose clothes, I **tend to think** of comfort first and appearance second.

b. verb + object + infinitive
Celebrities sometimes **inspire me to change** the way I look.

c. verb + gerund
I **hate choosing** my outfits in the morning.

d. verb + object + preposition + gerund
High prices rarely **prevent me from buying** quality clothing.

Grammar Plus: See page 108.

A Look at the starting point on page 10 again. Can you find another example of each pattern above?

B **Pair work** Which patterns from the box do these sentences follow? Write *a*, *b*, *c*, or *d*.

____ 1. I enjoy making a statement with my clothes.

____ 2. I like to wear unusual color combinations.

____ 3. I refuse to shop with my friends.

____ 4. I can't help being critical of what others wear.

____ 5. Parents should allow their children to wear whatever they want.

____ 6. My friends usually advise me against spending too much on clothes.

____ 7. My parents have always discouraged me from wearing sloppy clothes.

____ 8. Advertising definitely convinces me to buy certain articles of clothing.

C **Pair work** Which statements above are true for you? Explain and give examples.

D **Pair work** Complete each sentence below with a verb and your own ideas. Then add a follow-up comment, and compare with a partner.

advise	discourage	encourage	require	tend
allow	don't mind	permit	seem	try

1. Some schools still ____require____ students to wear ____school uniforms____ .
   They think that students will spend more time studying and less time thinking about clothes.

2. Parents often _____ their children from _____ .

3. Some restaurants don't _____ customers to _____ .

4. I _____ to wear clothes that _____ .

5. Experts _____ people against wearing _____ .

6. My clothes always _____ to make me look _____ .

7. I _____ buying expensive _____ .

8. Young people _____ to be concerned about _____ .

4. Your taste in clothes

vocabulary

A Look at the words below. Do some have similar meanings? Which ones would you use to describe your own style?

chic	conservative	fashionable	formal	functional	quirky	sloppy	stylish
classic	elegant	flashy	frumpy	funky	retro	stuffy	trendy

B **Pair work** What do you think of these styles?
Describe the people in the picture.

"Erica's outfit is pretty functional. She's clearly going to the gym."

"Really? I would say she's trendy. Jogging suits are really in fashion now for all occasions."

5. Fashion developments

listening

A **Pair work** Was your style the same five years ago? In what ways has your style changed? In what ways has it remained the same?

B 💿 Listen to Mark, Satoko, and Carlos describe how their tastes in fashion have changed. What was their style, and what is their style now?

	Then	Now
1. Mark		
2. Satoko		
3. Carlos		

C 💿 Listen again. Write the items of clothing or accessories you hear for each of the looks below.

grunge _____   bohemian _____

urban _____   sporty _____

goth _____   preppy _____

6 Writing about personal beliefs

writing

> In a composition about a personal belief, clearly state that belief in a thesis statement in the first paragraph. In the following paragraphs, give examples to support your thesis.

A Look at these fashion mottos. Which motto best reflects your opinion about fashion? Why? Share your ideas with a partner.

> **Don't just get dressed. Make a statement.**

> **Why look like everyone else?**

> **Feel comfortable. That's all that matters.**

> **Wear the very latest trends!**

B Use the motto you chose above as the basis for a thesis statement about your personal belief about fashion. Compare your ideas with a partner.

Your clothes should make a statement about who you are.

C Use your thesis statement to develop a composition of about 200 words in three paragraphs that describes your approach to clothes.

> I believe that clothes should be more than functional. They should make a statement about who you are. Before you get dressed or go shopping for clothing, it's important to think about what kind of message your clothes will send to others.
>
> I think of my clothes as a reflection of my personality. When people look at me and my clothes, they can get an idea of the kind of person I am. I'm interested in the arts, and I'm concerned about environmental issues. Therefore, I not only wear colorful clothes that are a bit unusual, but I also wear natural fabrics that are made locally. This is important to me.
>
> I don't follow trends because I don't like to look like everyone else. I'm unique, and I want my clothes to show it.

D **Pair work** Exchange compositions and answer these questions.

1. Does the idea in the first paragraph clearly state the writer's point of view?

2. Do the examples given in the other paragraphs support the thesis statement and clarify the writer's point of view?

3. What else do you want to know about your partner's attitude toward clothes?

Forming an impression

A Look at the statements about how people form a first impression of someone. Check (✓) the statements that are true for you.

First Impressions

WHAT PEOPLE NOTICE FIRST WHEN THEY MEET SOMEONE NEW

☐ I look at people's clothes first.

☐ What I notice is the other person's eyes.

☐ What's really important to me is a person's smile.

☐ What I always notice is a person's hands.

☐ I always appreciate a nice pair of shoes.

☐ What I notice is a person's figure (or physique).

☐ What strikes me first is the way people wear their hair.

☐ I have no idea what I notice first.

B **Group work** What other traits help you form an impression of a person? What are the three most important traits for the people in your group? Are they the same for men and women?

Important traits

A 💿 Listen to Gabriela, Joon, and Alice talk about traits that are important for them to form an impression, and complete the chart.

	Traits that are important to them
1. Gabriela	
2. Joon	
3. Alice	

B 💿 Listen again. Which of the speakers mentions traits that are *not* important to them? Which traits do they mention? Complete the chart.

	Traits that are not important to them
1. Gabriela	
2. Joon	
3. Alice	

C **Pair work** Which person is the most like you? Share your reasons with a partner.

grammar

> You can use *what* as the subject of the sentence when you want to emphasize information.
> This is called a cleft sentence.
> A person's smile **is really important to me**.   **What's really important to me is** a person's smile.
>
> **Use cleft sentences with verbs other than** *be* **by inserting** *what* **at the beginning of the sentence and a form of** *be* **after the main verb.**
> **I always notice** a person's hands.   **What I always notice is** a person's hands.
>
> *Grammar Plus: See page 109.*

A Look at the starting point on page 14 again. Can you find more cleft sentences? Try to change them into declarative sentences.

B Rewrite these sentences to add emphasis by beginning them with *what*. Which statements are true for you? Compare answers with a partner.

1. I appreciate a person with a good sense of humor.
   What I appreciate is a person with a good sense of humor.
2. I always notice the way people look at me.
3. A person's fashion sense is important to me.
4. I pay attention to people's manners.
5. I really dislike sarcasm.
6. I'm interested in the subjects people talk about.
7. A kind face is appealing to me.

No second chances

discussion

A Read these tips on making a good first impression. Then add one of your own, and choose the tip that you think is the most useful.

> ## QUICK TIPS for Making a Lasting Impression
>
> **1** Appearance matters. Dress a little nicer than you need to when meeting new people.
>
> **2** In a first conversation, use the other person's name from time to time, for example: *Katsuo, have you seen that new movie yet?* or *That's a good idea, Andrea.*
>
> **3** Good listening skills are the key to making a great first impression.
>
> **4** What you should do to make a positive first impression is show the other person that he or she is the center of the conversation, and not you.
>
> **5** Humor can be tricky. A little joke can be a nice way to break the ice, but what you should avoid is sarcasm.
>
> **6** _____
>
> _____

B **Group work** Share your choices and additional tips with the group. Then, as a group, try to agree on the three most useful tips.

"Well, if you want to make a good first impression, what matters most is your appearance."

"Maybe, but even if you look good, you still need to have something interesting to say."

5. Adjectives to describe outward appearance

vocabulary

A Which adjectives seem to have a positive meaning, a negative meaning, or a neutral meaning? Write +, –, or ~.

___ a. arrogant   ___ d. innocent   ___ g. sinister   ___ i. sympathetic

___ b. dignified   ___ e. intense   ___ h. smug   ___ j. trustworthy

___ c. eccentric   ___ f. intellectual

B Now match the words with their definitions. Write the correct letter.

1. deep in thought; contemplative ___
2. kind and understanding ___
3. worthy of respect or honor ___
4. reliable ___
5. forceful, with strong opinions ___
6. proud in an unpleasant way ___
7. self-satisfied; pleased with oneself ___
8. without blame; childlike and pure ___
9. strange or unusual in an amusing way ___
10. evil or ominous ___

C **Pair work** What famous people do the adjectives describe?

"To me, Johnny Depp looks intellectual."

"Oh, I don't know. He just looks eccentric, in my opinion."

6. Faces matter

discussion

Gisele Bündchen

Ken Watanabe

Drew Barrymore

Leonardo DiCaprio

Psychologist Leslie Zebrowitz found that people are usually categorized by their faces. She gave résumés of equally qualified people to groups of business students, with photos attached. It was discovered that the students recommended baby-faced people for jobs that required more sympathetic and submissive people, while people with mature faces were seen as more dignified or intense and were recommended for high-powered jobs, like lawyers. The study found that "more baby-faced people had baby-faced jobs. People seemed to be chosen for jobs, or to select themselves into jobs, to match their appearance."

Source: "Judging Faces Comes Naturally," by Jules Crittenden, Boston Herald

Pair work Answer these questions.

1. Which of the people above do you think have "baby faces"? What makes a baby face different from a mature face?

2. Name three well-known public figures who have tough jobs. Are they baby-faced, or do they have mature faces?

3 In some countries, job applications sometimes require a recent photo of the candidate. Do you agree with this practice? Why or why not?

7 Appearance and personality

A **Pair work** When meeting someone, what affects your impression of that person? Discuss with a partner. Then read the article.

First Impressions [COUNT]

Every time people make a new acquaintance, be it at a job interview, in primary school, parents' night, or at dinner with a friend's family, first impressions determine whether people consider each other likeable.

"More than half of a first impression is affected by appearance – clothes, makeup, body language, gestures, and facial expressions," said Mahena Stief, a business psychologist. But, it often makes a difference who the other person is. "I'm certain that when men judge women, appearance plays a greater role than when women judge other women," said Lydia Maier, chairwoman of an association of color and style advisers.

With the help of a mirror, a good female friend and a good male friend, one's own appearance can be thoroughly evaluated. Some important questions are: What effect do I have on you? Why is that so? Do I want to have that effect or something completely different?

The first place to look is in the closet. "Good clothes are not contingent upon how much was spent on them. What's important is that the clothes are neat, fit well, and match the personality of the person wearing them," said Maier. Depending on the occasion, choose a timeless, discreet, or stylish outfit for an introduction.

"Overall, the importance of fashion has increased in recent years," said professor Gerhard Amendt, director of an institute that conducts gender and generation research at the University of Bremen. He sees a danger, however, that the personality of a person could be lost behind a fashionable façade.

Well-being and inner stability are reflected in body language such as good posture, open expression, and smooth movements, and contribute to a positive appearance. People who are comfortable with themselves appear balanced and stable to others. "You can do a lot for your own well-being," said Stief. "It begins with clearing away major dissatisfactory things in your life." Relaxation exercises, yoga, or weight training promote balance. Exercising also helps people look healthy and energetic.

Expressive body language and gestures, appealing facial expressions, and communication skills can be learned by attending management seminars or adult education courses. No one becomes a perfect talk master through these means, but they help people recognize how others interpret their demeanor. "A considerable factor in appearance is self-confidence," said Amendt. "Only those people who are sure of themselves, who know their own strengths, and are convinced of them come across as self-confident and convincing."

Source: "First Impressions Count; appearance must match personality," by Eva Neumann

B Complete the sentences with information from the reading.

1. According to Mahena Stief, men put more emphasis on _____ .
2. Good clothes should match the wearer's _____ .
3. Good posture and smooth movements are a sign of _____ .
4. Communication skills can be improved by attending _____ seminars.

C **Group work** Discuss these questions. Then share your answers with the class.

1. What are some situations in which appearance is extremely important? Why?
2. Do you think your appearance generally matches your personality? Explain.
3. Do people of the opposite sex judge each other the same as those of their own sex?

LESSON A · Good science, bad science

What's new?

starting point

A Read about these advances in science. What are the possible benefits and dangers?

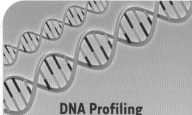

DNA Profiling

DNA profiles offer police a new way to fight crime. From any part of a person's body, a DNA profile can be identified. The development of the DNA profile has helped police identify criminals with great accuracy.

Artificial Intelligence

The best computer programs can drive cars, play chess, and even recognize emotions. In the future, artificial intelligence could have a huge impact on new technology in our daily lives, like personal robots.

Animal Cloning

Animal cloning begins with one cell from an animal — living, dead, or even extinct. From that cell, an exact copy of the animal can be created. The first animal cloned was a sheep, Dolly, in 1996.

B **Pair work** Read the information below about the scientific advances in Exercise A. Do you think each statement is a good idea (*G*) or a bad idea (*B*)? Discuss each statement with a partner.

____ 1. DNA profiles are taken from inmates in certain prisons in order to catch them if they commit future crimes.

_B_ 2. Companies are developing robots that can serve tea and take care of the elderly.

____ 3. Advocates have proposed creating a database of the DNA profiles of newborn infants.

_B_ 4. Governmental decision making could someday be turned over to computers.

_B_ 5. A company offers cloning of deceased pets for wealthy owners.

_G_ 6. Scientists are considering creating a clone from the frozen remains of an extinct mammoth.

The effects of technology

listening & speaking

A Listen to an interview about genetically modified food. What are some advantages of this technology? Write them in the chart.

Advantages	Disadvantages

B Listen again. What are some of the disadvantages? Complete the chart.

C **Pair work** Give an example of a new technology that has reshaped your daily life. What are the positive effects? What are the negative consequences?

3 Indefinite and definite articles

grammar

Review these rules for the indefinite articles *a* and *an* and the definite article *the*.

Countable nouns: Use an indefinite article (*a* or *an*) when you mention a singular countable noun for the first time, or no article for plural countable nouns. When you refer to the same item again, use *the*.
Animal cloning begins with one cell from **an animal** – living, dead, or even extinct. From that, an exact copy of **the animal** can be created.

If you use a plural noun to make a general statement, do not use an article. If you make the same statement using a singular noun, however, use *the*.
DNA profiles offer police a new way to fight crime.
The DNA profile offers police a new way to fight crime.

Uncountable nouns: When making a general statement, do not use an article with uncountable nouns (*technology, education, shopping, love*, etc.).
In the future, artificial **intelligence** could have a huge impact on our daily lives.

Superlative adjectives and sequence markers: Use *the* with superlatives and with sequence markers such as *first, last, next*, etc., but don't use *the* with time expressions such as *last night* or *next month*.
The best computer programs can drive cars, play chess, and even recognize emotions.

Grammar Plus: See page 110.

A Look at the starting point on page 18 again. Can you find another example of article usage for each rule in the grammar box?

B Complete these sentences with the correct article. Write X where none is needed.

1. _**X**_ Tracking technologies enable ___ websites to trace what online shoppers buy.

2. ___ DNA profiling of newborns was rejected in the United Kingdom in 2005.

3. ___ robot at Stanford University can use tools to successfully assemble ___ bookcase.

4. ___ first microbes able to consume oil were created to help clean up ___ oil spills.

5. *I, Robot* is the story of a battle between humans and robots – and ___ humans win!

6. I'm sure that a new computer will be even less expensive ___ next year.

7. ___ wireless technology makes the Internet available on a much wider scale.

8. For me, ___ blog is ___ most interesting innovation in news technology.

C Pair work Write statements about the items below. Then discuss your ideas with a partner.

1. the most interesting new product currently in stores
2. the most exciting new computer product on the market
3. the greatest advance in medicine
4. the most amazing invention of the twentieth century

"For me, the most interesting new product is the GPS navigation system."
"Oh, yeah. I have one in my car, and now I never get lost anymore."

4 A brave new world

vocabulary

A Match the words on the left with their definitions on the right.

1. audacious _c_   (*tonto*)   a. silly and wasteful; carelessly self-indulgent
2. confidential _d_   (*enredado*)   b. avoiding unnecessary risks
3. frivolous _a_   (*frivolo / audaz*)   c. bold and courageous when facing opposition (*valiente*)
4. hazardous _f_   d. private or secret
5. problematic _g_   e. against accepted beliefs about good behavior
6. prudent _b_   f. dangerous
7. unethical _e_   g. full of difficulties that are hard to solve

B Complete the sentences with the words above. Then compare your answers with a partner. Sometimes more than one answer is possible.

1. Sadly, much of our _confidential_ personal information is now on the Internet.

2. Though intelligent robots appear in many movies, creating a real one is extremely _problematic_ , and probably impossible with today's technology.

3. Some cautious people don't think it is _prudent_ to use a credit card to shop online.

4. Many people feel it is _unethical_ for companies to spy on employees' e-mail.

5. The space shuttle disasters of 1986 and 2003 show how _hazardous_ space travel is. _or problematic_

6. The doctor needed to be _frivolous_ to speak out against DNA profiling when most of his audience was for it.

7. With thousands of dogs and cats looking for homes, cloning additional ones for pets seems _audacious_ .

5 Pros and cons

discussion

Group work Look at these newspaper headlines. Discuss the positive effects and negative consequences of the events in the headlines. *Titulares*

Plastic Surgery Better and Cheaper Than Ever

Many men and women today are considering

Farmers Plant Genetically Engineered Crops to Save Money

Cultivos

"I'm a bit leery of plastic surgery. It seems like everyone's doing it these days."

"Well, I'm all for it if it makes people happy."

Internet peaks as most important information source

Picos   *Fuente*

Online technology has surpassed all other

Microchip Implant Allows Criminals to Be Followed 24 Hours a Day

There is a debate over whether or not

Useful expressions

Expressing caution and confidence
I'm a bit leery of . . .
You should think twice about . . .
I'm all for . . .
I have every confidence that . . .

6. Writing summaries

writing

> When you write a summary, state in your own words the main points of a text, leaving out most of the supporting details. The summary must accurately reflect the ideas of the original text.

A Read the passage and underline the main points.

ANIMAL CLONING
BENEFITS AND CONCERNS

Animal cloning is the technique of creating an exact genetic copy of an animal from a single cell. It has previously been used to create copies of, for example, sheep, cows, and cats. While animal cloning is an amazing and powerful technology with possible benefits to science and humanity, many people are voicing concerns about the ethics and wisdom of this scientific innovation.

On the surface, animal cloning simply seems to be the "copying" of an animal, and it is difficult to see the benefits. However, the potential benefits of animal cloning are many. Cloned animals can be useful in the production of certain drugs to treat human illnesses. Through cloning, scientists can modify animal organs, such as heart valves, so that they can be safely transplanted into the human body. Cloning could also be very useful in the saving of endangered species. Two types of Asian cattle, the gaur and the banteng, have been helped in this way. Furthermore, cloning can be used to produce animals that are unable to reproduce naturally, such as mules.

Those who argue against cloning warn of its dangers. Organs transplanted from animals to humans are not always safe, and there is a risk of disease. Additionally, for every animal that is successfully cloned, there are frequently a number of others produced that are not healthy enough to live, and cloned animals themselves can be weaker than those from normal reproduction. When it comes to saving endangered animals, critics argue that cloning is too expensive and takes the attention and resources away from the real problem – the destruction of animal habitat.

In conclusion, it seems clear that the differences between the two sides of the animal cloning issue will not easily come to agreement. But, as scientific progress presents us with new technologies such as animal cloning, it is important to discuss their benefits and voice our concerns about their use.

B Read the summary below. What main points were left out from the original passage?

Summary

Animal cloning is a technique for creating a copy of an animal from a single cell. People who support animal cloning argue that it can be useful in the production of drugs and transplant organs for humans. They also point out its value in preserving endangered species. Those who are against it argue that its medical uses are actually unsafe, that it produces unhealthy animals, and that it distracts us from the real problems that endangered animals face.

C **Pair work** Choose your own article on technology or a related topic. Then choose an important paragraph, and write the main idea. Compare with a partner.

D Write a summary of all or part of the article in one or more paragraphs.

1 Terrible technology

starting point

A Read about three people who had trouble with technology. How would you have felt in their situation? What would you have done?

Stan, 26

" Having completed a 20-page story for my creative writing class, I clicked 'print.' Well, my computer crashed printing the first page! Finally at 10 P.M., having tried everything to fix the computer, I started rewriting the story – by hand. It took me most of the night! "

Peter, 17

" Being a curious person, I once decided to search the Web for my own name. Not many search results came up, but one labeled 'geeks' caught my eye. Looking at the site, I almost died! It was my face – a classmate had posted it! I e-mailed the website, and they took it off the next day. "

Vera, 36

" My boss asked me to give a presentation to some clients. Being a perfectionist, I prepared it in detail on my laptop. The next day, I took the clients into a room, turned on my laptop, and . . . nothing! Trying to stay calm, I gave the presentation as best I could from memory. "

B **Pair work** What technology gives you the most trouble? Tell your partner a story of a time you had trouble with technology.

"Sometimes I have trouble with e-mail. I remember one day I had over 100 spam messages . . ."

2 I can't cope with it!

listening

A Listen to a comedian talk about the difficulties he has coping with the technology in his house. Write the items he mentions in the chart.

Items	Problems

B Listen again. What does he find exasperating about each item? Complete the chart.

3 -ing clauses

grammar

To express two actions performed by the same person or thing in a single sentence, we can include an *-ing* clause. An *-ing* clause contains an *-ing* participle.

The two actions happen at the same time or one action happens during another action.
My computer crashed **printing** the first page.
(My computer crashed *while/when* it was printing the very first page.)

Trying to stay calm, I gave the presentation as best I could from memory.
(I was trying to stay calm *while* I gave the presentation as best I could from memory.)

She is at her desk **typing a paper**.
(She is at her desk *and* she is typing a paper.)

When one action happens before another action, use *having* + past participle.
Having completed a 20-page story for my creative writing class, I clicked "print."

Reasons and explanations for actions can be expressed with *-ing* clauses.
Being a curious person, I once decided to search the Web for my own name.
(*Because* I am a curious person, . . .)

Grammar Plus: See page 111.

A Look at the starting point again on page 22. Can you find more examples of *-ing* clauses in the stories?

B Combine the sentences using an *-ing* clause. Then compare answers with a partner.

1. I forgot my password. I couldn't access my e-mail until a friend helped me.

   Having forgotten my password, I couldn't access my e-mail until a friend helped me.

2. My computer ran out of memory. It was downloading a large file.

3. I am very clumsy. I tripped and broke my MP3 player.

4. I opened a strange e-mail attachment yesterday. I started having computer problems.

5. Harry was using his DVR. Harry recorded all his favorite TV shows.

6. The police implanted the criminal with a microchip. The police easily tracked him to his hideout.

7. Wen learned about camera phones. Wen was reading *TechToday* magazine.

8. Mari just got her first cell phone. Mari now calls her friends ten times a day.

C **Pair work** Complete the sentences with your own ideas. Compare answers with a partner.

1. Having broken my . . .

   cell phone, I no longer have anyone's phone number.

2. Being a creative person, . . .

3. Trying to keep up with new technologies, . . .

4. Having purchased a new . . .

Different attitudes

A Look at these expressions. Which ones express a positive attitude, a negative attitude, or a neutral attitude? Write +, –, or ~.

____ 1. aware of   ____ 5. familiar with   ____ 9. crazy about

____ 2. curious about   ____ 6. suspicious of   ____ 10. reliant on

____ 3. sick of   ____ 7. intimidated by   ____ 11. grateful for

____ 4. fed up with   ____ 8. knowledgeable about   ____ 12. leery of

B **Group work** Look at the list of inventions and technologies. Can you think of more? What are your feelings about them? Discuss with the class.

1. video surveillance
2. handheld computers/PDAs
3. voice recognition software
4. digital photography
5. laser surgery
6. MP3 players
7. cell phones
8. robots

"So, what do you think about video surveillance in the city?"

"I'm not sure. It's kind of an invasion of privacy."

Tech savvy?

A Are you a technophile or a technophobe? Complete the survey to find out.

TECHNOPHILE *or* TECHNOPHOBE?

	Not Sure (1 pt.)	Agree (2 pts.)	Disagree (0 pts.)
1. If technology permits it, I would favor the development of machines that surpass humans in intelligence.	☐	☐	☐
2. Nuclear energy is clean, safe, and reliable.	☐	☐	☐
3. Everyone should try to stay informed about the latest innovations in technology.	☐	☐	☐
4. Genetic technologies should be used to gradually improve the human body over the course of generations.	☐	☐	☐
5. Science and technology will someday solve all the world's problems.	☐	☐	☐
6. I trust scientists and the government to make sure powerful new technologies are used wisely.	☐	☐	☐
7. I couldn't do without computers or computerized devices.	☐	☐	☐
8. It's important for everyone to be connected to the Internet.	☐	☐	☐

SCORE

0–4 You are a technophobe, a person who has a strong mistrust of technology.

5–8 While not in love with technology, you see the need for it in our world.

9–12 You're a fan of technology and may be showing some signs of being a geek.

13–16 You're a technophile, a person who is crazy about technology.

B **Group work** Discuss your answers to the survey. Talk about the reasons for your choices and whether or not you agree with your score.

6. The Amish

reading

A **Pair work** What do you know about the Amish? What is their attitude toward technology? Discuss with a partner. Then read the article.

WHO ARE THE AMISH?

On the surface, many Amish look like they stepped out of the rural 19th century. The most conservative group of Amish are known as "Old Order Amish." They drive horses and buggies rather than cars. Many have no telephones or electricity in their homes. They send their children to private, one-room schoolhouses until the age of 13. They eschew technology and do not join the military or accept assistance from the government.

The Amish community in Lancaster County, Pennsylvania, was a model for the 1985 film *Witness* starring Harrison Ford, a thriller which contrasted the violent modern world with their peaceful existence. Actually, the Amish experience many of the same problems as other communities, but keep them private.

STRICT REGULATIONS

Some 200,000 Amish people live in more than 20 U.S. states and in the Canadian province of Ontario. The oldest group of Old Order Amish, about 16,000–18,000 people, live in Lancaster County, a rural, farming area where Amish first settled in the 1720s – many fleeing persecution in Europe.

The Amish are divided into dozens of separate fellowships, broken down into districts or congregations. Each district is fully independent and lives by its own set of unwritten rules, or *Ordnung*. The Old Order are the most conservative of these groups and observe strict regulations on dress, behavior, and the use of technology, which they believe encourage humility and separation from the world.

Old Order Amish women wear modest dresses with long sleeves and a full skirt, a cape, and an apron. They never cut their hair, but wear it in a bun on the back of the head. Men and boys wear dark-colored suits, straight-cut coats, and black or straw broad-brimmed hats. They grow beards only after they marry.

Modern technology is not rejected out of hand. Some farms have telephones, and local groups can allow electricity to be used in certain circumstances.

Most Amish are trilingual. They speak a dialect of German called Pennsylvania Dutch at home, use High German at special events, and they learn English at school.

In some ways, the Amish are feeling the pressures of the modern world. Commentators say child labor laws, for example, are threatening long-established ways of life.

Source: "Who are the Amish?" BBC News

B What is the Amish approach to each of these areas of life?

1. transportation
2. education
3. government
4. community problems
5. electricity
6. appearance
7. telephones
8. languages

C **Group work** Discuss these questions. Then share your answers with the class.

1. Why do you think the Amish continue their alternative lifestyle?
2. What do you think the Amish do for fun?
3. Could you live among the Amish? Why or why not?

Self-assessment

How well can you do these things? Rate your ability from 1 to 5 (1 = low, 5 = high).

Listen for gerund and infinitive constructions in a conversation (Ex. 1)   _____

Listen to adjectives and phrasal verbs to describe people and styles (Ex. 1)   _____

Talk about different attitudes toward fashion using cleft sentences (Ex. 2)   _____

Discuss technological issues using definite and indefinite articles (Ex. 3)   _____

Express opinions about the positive and negative effects of technology (Ex. 4)   _____

Now do the corresponding exercises below. Were your ratings correct?

1 Class reunion

listening

A Listen to a conversation between two friends. What is Karla trying to do? Check (✓) the correct answer.

☐ a. She's planning to set up a fashion website.

☐ b. She's using a website to organize a class reunion.

☐ c. She's calling her ex-classmates.

B Listen again. Are these statements true or false? Check (✓) the correct answer.

	True	False
1. Karla is intimidated by the website technology.	☐	☐
2. Lucy isn't sure that a reunion would be completely harmonious.	☐	☐
3. Neither woman liked Andrew very much.	☐	☐
4. Renee's fashion taste has changed since she was in high school.	☐	☐
5. Javier's style has changed since he was in high school.	☐	☐

2 Fashion statements

speaking

A Which of these statements about clothing do you agree with most?

- What you wear is who you are.
- People often discriminate against others because of the way they dress.
- Buying new clothes all the time is unethical.
- Clothes are like art that you wear.
- People who are interested in fashion are shallow and superficial.

B **Group work** Join another group and compare your results. Try to find two statements that you all agree with.

3. Technological advances

discussion

A Which of these advances in technology has had the most positive or negative impact on our lives?

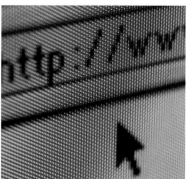
Internet technology

internal combustion engine

genetically modified food

large scale farming

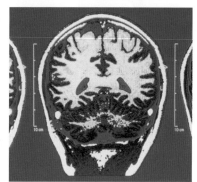
medical technology

atomic power

B **Pair work** Compare your answers with a partner.

"I think the Internet has had the most positive impact on our lives. We have access to so much more information than we did twenty, or even ten years ago."

"Well, that's true, but medical technology has had a really positive influence on more people around the world."

4. Is technology good or bad?

discussion

A Read these opinions about technology. What are the main issues they raise? What's your own point of view on these issues?

When you are ready to invest in a new technology, there are a few questions you should ask yourself. First, is the new item cheaper than what it replaces? Does it save space? Will it make your life easier? Is it energy efficient? Can you repair it inexpensively? If not, don't buy it.

— Dong Hyun, Pusan, Korea

How we think about technology is flawed. We are over-eager to have the newest gadget. We are too impressed by speed, noise, compactness, and general flashiness. We need a more mature and cautious way of thinking about technology. New is not always better.

— Inés Candia, Asuncion, Paraguay

B **Group work** Compare your ideas. Are your points of view similar? How?

1 The things people believe!

A Read the list of superstitions. Do you believe in any of them?

Beliefs Across Cultures

In Turkey, many people agree that when someone goes on a journey, you should pour water on the ground behind him or her to bring the person back safely.

In Brazil, people claim you should enter a place using your right foot to have good fortune.

In Russia, looking into a broken mirror will bring bad luck.

In Argentina, many people believe that if you drop a coin into a fountain, you can ask for three wishes to come true.

In Japan, it is very bad luck to give a present that consists of four pieces.

In Venezuela, some people say that if someone passes a broom over your feet, you will never get married.

In Greece, the crow is a very unlucky animal. If you see a crow in the morning, it means that you will have a bad day.

B Pair work Which superstitions do some people in your culture believe?

2 Expressions with *luck*

A Match the statements with the replies containing *luck*.

1. "I've got to go. I have a big test tomorrow." ____
2. "I'm out of cash. Is there an ATM nearby?" ____
3. "He won the first game of chess he ever played!" ____
4. "He lost his job and house, and now he's sick." ____
5. "Are you going to Europe this summer?" ____
6. "How did you win those soccer tickets?" ____
7. "Thanks for the $20. Can I have $40 more?" ____

a. "That was beginner's luck."
b. "No such luck. I'm staying home."
c. "I'm afraid you're out of luck."
d. "Wow! He's got bad luck."
e. "Well, best of luck!"
f. "Don't push your luck."
g. "It was the luck of the draw."

B Pair work Use the expressions with *luck* to write short dialogues. Act them out with your partner.

"I really want tickets to the John Mayer concert."

"I'm afraid you're out of luck. They sold out in 10 minutes!"

3 Reporting clauses

grammar

> To report what someone says, thinks, believes, etc., you can use a sentence that includes
> a reporting clause.
>
> In Turkey, **many people agree (that)** when someone goes on a journey, you should pour water on the ground
> behind him or her to bring the person back safely.
>
> In Venezuela, **some people say (that)** if someone passes a broom over your feet, you will never get married.
>
> The use of the word *that* in these clauses is optional. The following verbs are often used
> in reporting clauses.
> **More formal**: argue   assert   claim   report
> **More conversational**: admit   agree   assume   believe   doubt   explain   feel   say
>
> **Grammar Plus:** *See page 112.*

A Look at the starting point on page 28 again. Can you find the sentences that
contain reporting clauses? For those that don't, add a reporting clause and
rewrite the sentence.

B Rewrite each sentence with a reporting clause. Use a different reporting verb
to introduce each one.

1. Everyone is superstitious about a few things.

   *Many people agree that almost everyone
   is superstitious about a few things.*

2. It's fine to follow superstitions for fun,
   but not to really believe in them.

3. Superstitions are an important part of our
   cultural heritage.

4. Superstitions are dangerous because
   they prevent people from thinking
   scientifically.

5. Behind many holiday rituals, you can
   find ancient beliefs and superstitions.

6. Superstitions sometimes contain truths
   handed down from the past.

C **Pair work** Share your answers above with your partner. Then give your
opinions about the statements.

*"Many people agree that almost everyone is superstitious about a few things. It's true! When
I spill some salt, I always throw a little over my left shoulder so I don't have bad luck."*

4 Everyday superstitions

discussion

A **Pair work** Do you know any superstitions connected with these things?

- animals
- clothing
- colors
- days, dates, or months
- food
- household objects
- money
- numbers
- weddings

B **Group work** Join another pair and compare your
answers. Ask follow-up questions.

*"In Russia, it is customary to smash the glasses after you
give a toast to the bride and groom."*

"Really? Why is that?"

*"Well, some people believe it will bring happiness
to their marriage."*

5. Common explanations

listening

A Listen to people talk about superstitions. What superstitions are they talking about? What is an explanation for each superstition?

B Listen again. Answer these questions.

1. How did the woman with the allergies react to the man's explanation?
2. Why did the son feel it was necessary to say that he was only kidding?
3. Why does the man suggest not telling Mr. Wilson that being left-handed was once thought to be suspicious?

6. Are you superstitious?

discussion

A **Pair work** Take turns interviewing each other, and complete the questionnaire. Then calculate your scores.

Lucky or Unlucky?

		YES (1 pt.)	NO (0 pt.)
1.	Is it unlucky not to say something like "bless you" when someone sneezes?	☐	☐
2.	Are there any particular days that you consider unlucky?	☐	☐
3.	Do you have any lucky numbers?	☐	☐
4.	Do you think some colors bring good luck?	☐	☐
5.	Do you avoid walking under a ladder because it might bring you bad luck?	☐	☐
6.	Are there any animals you consider unlucky?	☐	☐
7.	Do you believe that certain actions before a wedding bring good or bad luck?	☐	☐
8.	Do you carry any good luck charms or have any in your house?	☐	☐
9.	Do you have a piece of clothing that brings you good luck?	☐	☐
10.	Do you avoid having specific items in your house because they might bring bad luck?	☐	☐

SCORE

0–1 Life is not a matter of luck to you!
2–4 You're not very superstitious, but . . .

5–7 You're fairly superstitious, aren't you?
8–10 Wow! You're really superstitious!

B **Group work** Compare your scores. Then explain some of the things you're superstitious about. Is there anything else that you think brings good or bad luck?

"Well, when I talk about something that's going well, I say 'knock on wood.'"
"Really? Why do you do that?"
"Well, they say that if you knock on something made of wood, your luck will continue."

7. Restating a thesis

writing

> The first paragraph of a composition provides the thesis statement and sometimes gives general examples. The last paragraph restates the thesis statement.

A Read this composition. Find the thesis statement and a supporting example in the first paragraph. Then look at the last paragraph. Which sentence restates the thesis statement?

SUPERSTITIONS: Hard to Ignore

Some people think that certain objects bring them good luck; others avoid certain things or situations that they believe might bring them bad luck. Even people who claim not to believe in superstitions sometimes use phrases such as "knock on wood" when they speak. Superstitions concerning both good and bad luck are part of everyone's life in the United States. Even if you don't believe in them, they are difficult to ignore.

It's easy to find superstitions relating to good luck. For example, my friend Irene carries a rabbit's foot in her pocket to bring her good luck. Another friend who plays baseball panics whenever his mother washes his "lucky" baseball socks. My mother believes that nine is her lucky number, and even my level-headed father has hung a horseshoe over the entrance of our home to bring us good luck and good fortune.

Superstitions concerning bad luck are just as common. My mother believes that certain days are bad for events like marriages and ceremonies, while my uncle always says "knock on wood" and then looks for something made of wood to knock on with his hand. Then there's my friend who goes out of his way to avoid black cats. My sister never puts her bag on the floor because she thinks doing so will bring her bad luck.

Personally, I am not very superstitious. I don't have any lucky socks, and I don't have any lucky or unlucky numbers. Still, I find myself avoiding black cats and knocking on wood every now and then. Superstitions are just a part of life, whether or not you believe them.

B Write a composition about superstitions and good and bad luck in your culture. Do your first and last paragraphs follow the guidelines stated in the box?

C **Pair work** Exchange your composition with a partner, and answer these questions.

1. Does the first paragraph contain a thesis statement and give general examples?

2. How well do the examples in the middle paragraphs support the thesis? Are there enough examples?

3. Does the last paragraph restate the thesis?

1. Fact or fiction?

starting point

A Three of these news stories are true and one is false. Decide which one is false.

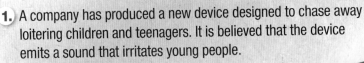

1. A company has produced a new device designed to chase away loitering children and teenagers. It is believed that the device emits a sound that irritates young people.

2. Dog Island is a paradise for dogs. Dog owners are encouraged to set their dogs free there and allow them to live out their lives without humans or leashes.

3. A candy company is selling lollipops with a variety of insects inside, including crickets, ants, and scorpions. It is claimed that the lollipops are actually quite tasty.

4. It's been reported that a website continuously broadcasts videos of wheels of cheddar cheese as they ripen. It is believed that a video of one single wheel can continue for months or years.

B **Pair work** Tell your partner your choice and explain why you think it is false. (For the answer, turn to page 152.)

2. That sounds fishy!

vocabulary & speaking

A Which of these words describe the truth, and which describe something fabricated? Divide them into two groups. Then add two more items to each group.

believable	convincing	dubious	fishy	misleading	plausible
conceivable	credible	far-fetched	iffy	phony	well-founded

B Use the words above to write about each story in the starting point.

The article about the candy company sounds completely phony to me. It's just not a plausible story.

C **Group work** Take turns making statements, some true and some false, about yourself to your partner. Respond using the words describing truth and fabrication.

"I have a very good singing voice, and I sing with a band on the weekend."

"Well your speaking voice is very nice, so that seems pretty believable to me."

3 Reporting clauses in the passive

grammar

To report a general claim or opinion, you can use a passive form of a reporting verb and *it*.
Notice that the agent is often omitted and understood to be "some people" or "many people."
It is believed (**that**) the device emits a sound that irritates young people.
It is claimed (**that**) the lollipops are actually quite tasty.

Grammar Plus: See page 113.

A Look at the starting point on page 32 again. Can you find another example of a reporting clause in the passive?

B Rewrite these statements with a reporting clause in the passive with *it*.

1. People estimate that 50 percent of the population believes in ghosts.

   It is estimated that 50 percent of the population believes in ghosts.

2. Someone has said that the only time people don't want to hear gossip is when the gossip is about them.

3. Many claim that some people can communicate with plants.

4. People once thought the sun moved around the earth.

5. Some sources have reported that practical jokes on April 1 are becoming less common.

6. Experts argue that people create e-mail hoaxes for a wide variety of reasons.

7. Sociologists think that in the days before television, folktales were an important form of family entertainment.

8. People too easily assume that just because something is in print, it's true.

C **Pair work** Use reporting clauses in the passive to talk about these amazing facts.

1. A heart-shaped potato was grown in Idaho.
2. A 33-year-old man married a 104-year-old woman.
3. On April 1, 2006, a flight was denied permission to land because the air traffic controller was on a tea break.
4. There is a company that sells a seven-person bicycle.
5. You can send a coconut through the mail in the United States without any wrapping.
6. Istanbul, Turkey, is the only city in the world located on two continents.
7. The hottest pepper in the world, the Dorset Naga, was developed in England.

"Get this – it's been reported that a heart-shaped potato was grown in Idaho."

Useful expressions

Reporting something surprising
Get this – . . .
Believe it or not, . . .
Did you hear what happened?

D **Pair work** Complete these statements about beliefs using your own information. Compare your statements with a partner.

1. People don't believe this anymore, but it used to be said that . . .
2. Recently, it has been reported in the news that . . .

4 Shocking news

listening

A Look at the map of Belgium. What do you know about this country? What languages do Belgians speak?

B  Listen to a conversation about a TV hoax that affected many people in Belgium. What was happening to Belgium, according to the hoax broadcast?

C Listen again. Which events actually happened? Check (✓) the correct answers.

☐ 1. The king and queen left the country.

☐ 2. The Belgian flag was lowered over government buildings.

☐ 3. Internet servers crashed all over the country.

☐ 4. Foreign government officials called their home countries.

5 Internet hoaxes

discussion

A **Pair work** Have you ever read or heard about something on the Internet that was a hoax? Tell your partner about it.

B **Pair work** Read these claims found on the Internet. Check (✓) the ones you think are hoaxes. (For the answers, turn to page 152.) Then discuss with a partner.

WEBSITE CLAIMS   HOAX?

1. A man offers $10,000 to anyone who can find him a wife.	◯
2. Chewing gum takes seven years to pass through the human digestive system.	◯
3. A website called "The End of the Internet" claims to be the final page on the Internet.	◯
4. There is a monkey that is able to communicate with humans by typing on a keyboard.	◯
5. An 85-year-old woman is training to climb Mount Everest with her little dog.	◯
6. The Childhood Goat Trauma Foundation helps adults who were terrified by goats at a young age.	◯
7. "Pets by Mail" lets you order pets online and have them delivered to your home.	◯
8. Lacuna, Inc., is a company that will painlessly erase your troubling memories.	◯

C **Group work** Discuss these questions with your group.

1. Which of the website claims seems the most plausible to you? Which seems the most iffy?

2. Why do you think people create hoax websites and hoax e-mails?

3. Do you think people who create Internet hoaxes should be punished?

6. The killing stone

reading

A **Pair work** Do you think certain items bring bad luck to their owners? Discuss with a partner. Then read the article.

The Legend of the Hope Diamond

Of the entire world's big diamonds, the most infamous is known as the Hope diamond, a blue-colored beauty dubbed "The Killing Stone." The legend, which has many variations, began in 1666 when a French trader named Jean-Baptiste Tavernier plucked it from the eye of a statue in India. This gave birth to the legendary curse when wild dogs tore him apart just after he had sold the diamond. His was the first horrible death attributed to the deadly curse.

The businessman who had acquired the stone from Tavernier sold it to King Louis XIV and soon caught a mysterious disease and died. King Louis XIV had the 115-carat diamond cut into a heart shaped 69-carat stone, and it was passed down to Louis XVI and his wife Marie Antoinette. According to legend, Marie Antoinette and Louis XVI were beheaded during the French Revolution because of the diamond's curse.

After the French Revolution, the diamond was hidden in a government building, where it was stolen in 1791. Forty years later, it reappeared in London, and Henry Philip Hope purchased it at an auction. Hope soon suffered an unexplained death, and his wife burned to death in their mansion. The following years found the diamond in possession of a number of cursed owners: a Russian prince who killed his girlfriend, a Greek whose family died when their car drove off a cliff, and a Turkish sultan who also killed his girlfriend.

Finally, in 1949, famous New York jeweler Harry Winston bought the diamond. To rid himself of the curse, Winston sent the magnificent blue diamond in a plain brown box to the Smithsonian Institution in Washington, D.C., where it has remained ever since.

In 2003, the Hope diamond was taken to a laboratory for testing. Scientists focused an ultraviolet light beam on the stone, and when they turned it off, the diamond glowed bright orange-amber – most blue diamonds glow light blue. Some say that the color reflects the trail of blood and bad luck that has followed the stone over the centuries. Yet, the Hope diamond has been nothing but good luck for the Smithsonian. It is the most famous museum piece in the world, with over 5 million people viewing it each year.

Source: "The Infamous Hope Diamond," by G. L. Bycz, finejewelrydesigns.com

B **Pair work** Number the events in the correct order. Then compare with a partner. Take turns providing more details about each part of the story.

____ a. The diamond is sold to Henry Philip Hope.

____ b. A businessman buys it and sells it to a French king.

____ c. A trader steals the diamond in India.

____ d. Scientists test the stone and find it glows orange-amber.

____ e. Harry Winston buys the diamond and donates it to the Smithsonian Institution.

____ f. The diamond reappears at a London auction after almost 40 years.

C **Group work** Discuss these questions. Then share your answers with the class.

1. Do you think there's any truth to the legends surrounding the Hope diamond? Explain.

2. If someone offered you the Hope diamond as a gift, would you accept it? Why or why not?

Television and reading

LESSON A · Television

1 What's On?

starting point

A Read these blog posts about TV programs. Which program would you like most to watch? Which one would least interest you? Why?

What's On?
A television-themed blog

Posted at 3:07 p.m. by Nick
Lost is such a cool show. It's filmed in Oahu, Hawaii, but it's a drama about the adventures of a group of people whose plane crashes on a remote island in the South Pacific. It has such a big cast that it's one of TV's most expensive shows to make. My friends and I are such big fans that it's all we talk about when we get together!

Posted at 2:48 p.m. by Mayu
These days there are so few good shows on television that I rarely watch it anymore. But I never miss Star Academy. It's a singing competition and reality TV show all in one, and it's broadcast in over 50 countries! The winners are so talented that they often become successful in the music industry. But even the losers are great. They all do so much work to prepare for their final performances. I just can't stop watching.

Posted at 2:31 p.m. by Shane
There are so many crime drama series on TV that I get them all confused. And we all have so little free time that we can't waste it watching mediocre shows. The one I recommend is Law & Order. The acting is great, and the cast is really good-looking. Plus, the storylines are so gripping that you slip into another world!

B Pair work What are your favorite TV programs? What do you like about them?

"I'm really into this Mexican soap opera. The plot has lots of surprises, and the storyline is so creative."

2 Types of TV programs

vocabulary

A Pair work Look at the different types of TV programs. Check (✓) the ones that you know. Then ask a partner about the ones you don't know.

- ☐ 1. game show
- ☐ 2. soap opera
- ☐ 3. reality TV
- ☐ 4. cartoon
- ☐ 5. documentary
- ☐ 6. drama series
- ☐ 7. sports program
- ☐ 8. talk show
- ☐ 9. sketch comedy show
- ☐ 10. cooking show
- ☐ 11. sitcom (situational comedy)
- ☐ 12. news program

B Group work Which types of TV shows do you watch? Can you name an example of each type of program above?

3 *Such . . . that* and *so . . . that*

grammar

So and *such*, *such . . . that*, *so . . . that*, *so much/little . . . that*, and *so many/few . . . that* are commonly used to express extremes in exclamatory sentences.

a. ***Such*** is followed by a noun (usually modified by an adjective).
It has **such** a big cast **that** it's one of TV's most expensive shows to make.

b. ***So*** is followed by an adjective or adverb.
The storylines are **so** gripping **that** you slip into another world!

c. ***So many*** and ***so few*** are followed by countable nouns.
There are **so few** good shows on television **that** I rarely watch it anymore.

d. ***So much*** and ***so little*** are followed by uncountable nouns.
We all have **so little** free time **that** we can't waste it.

Grammar Plus: See page 114.

A Look at the starting point on page 36 again. Can you find more sentences with *so* and *such*? Which patterns do the sentences follow?

B Complete these sentences with *so many*, *so few*, *so much*, or *so little*.

1. My brother watches ___so much___ TV that he hardly does anything else.

2. There are _____ *American Idol* fans that it's consistently the highest rated show on American TV.

3. There was _____ interest in the cartoon that the network canceled it.

4. I have bought _____ DVDs that I now need to buy a new cabinet.

5. In my town, there are _____ television channels that some people buy satellite dishes to widen the selection.

6. There's a new drama series that features _____ good acting that I sometimes forget it's not real.

C Rewrite these sentences using *such . . . that* or *so . . . that*. Make any other necessary changes. Then compare with a partner.

1. Documentaries today deal with real issues. More and more people are watching them.

   Documentaries today deal with such real issues that more and more people are watching them.

2. There are many channels available on cable TV. I find it difficult to choose what to watch.

3. Endorsing products is well paid. Many celebrities are now selling products on TV.

4. Certain singers attract huge audiences. They charge more for concert tickets.

5. Commercials are much longer than the TV shows. I just watch TV on the Internet now to avoid them.

4 Popular TV programs

listening

A 🎧 Listen to these critics talk about some popular TV shows in the United States. Write the type of program beside each title.

1. *The Oprah Winfrey Show* _____
2. *As the World Turns* _____
3. *Ugly Betty* _____
4. *Cash Cab* _____

B 🎧 Listen again. Why is each program so successful? Complete the chart.

	Reasons for success
1. *The Oprah Winfrey Show*	
2. *As the World Turns*	
3. *Ugly Betty*	
4. *Cash Cab*	

C **Pair work** Make a list of three popular TV shows, and discuss the reasons why these programs are so popular.

"The Simpsons is a really popular cartoon. I think people like it because it uses humor to make you think about some of the problems in today's world. So it's funny, but it's serious too."

5 Conflicting views on television

discussion

A Read these comments on the positive and negative influences of television. Can you think of additional influences?

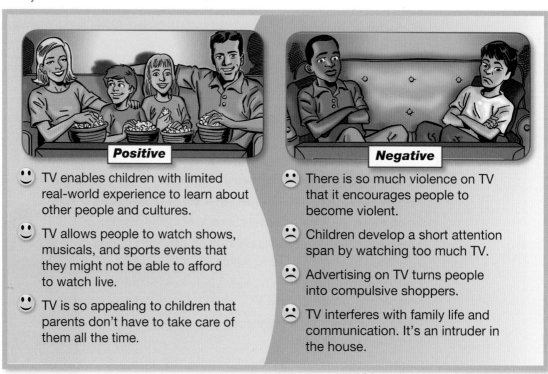

Positive

🙂 TV enables children with limited real-world experience to learn about other people and cultures.

🙂 TV allows people to watch shows, musicals, and sports events that they might not be able to afford to watch live.

🙂 TV is so appealing to children that parents don't have to take care of them all the time.

Negative

🙁 There is so much violence on TV that it encourages people to become violent.

🙁 Children develop a short attention span by watching too much TV.

🙁 Advertising on TV turns people into compulsive shoppers.

🙁 TV interferes with family life and communication. It's an intruder in the house.

B **Group work** Discuss the comments. Give reasons why you think they are positive or negative.

Writing a review of a TV program

writing

An effective review of a TV program generally provides information about the program, summarizes a particular episode, and offers a recommendation based on the writer's opinion.

A Read the questions and the TV review below. Circle the answers to the questions in the review and write the number of the question.

1. What is the title of the program, and what type of show is it?

2. What made you decide to watch the program, and what is your general impression?

3. What is the program about?

4. Who are the main characters and actors?

5. Why is the show worth watching?

6. Would you recommend this program to others? Why or why not?

1

TELEVISION REVIEW: EVERYBODY HATES CHRIS

Last week I watched such an enjoyable episode of the hilarious sitcom *Everybody Hates Chris*.

I tuned in because my favorite comedian, Chris Rock, narrates this program about his childhood in Brooklyn, New York, during the early 1980s. I was not disappointed.

The part of young Chris is played so convincingly by the young actor Tyler James Williams, who is wise beyond his years. Rochelle (Tichina Arnold) is Chris's strict but loving mother, who runs the household. Julius (Terry Crews) is the father who works multiple jobs to provide for his family and who is such a strong role model for Chris and his younger brother Drew (Tequan Richmond) and sister Tonya (Imani Hakim).

Everybody Hates Chris is a perfect TV program, and the characters are so memorable. It reminds me of *The Cosby Show*, one of my all-time favorite TV programs, but Chris has a spirit

all its own. It's great to see a sitcom that the entire family can watch together and that has kids acting like kids, not 12-year-olds talking like 30-year-olds.

Check out *Everybody Hates Chris* with your family tonight at 8 P.M. You won't regret it!

B Think of a TV program you've seen recently, and make notes to answer the six questions above. Then use your notes to write a review of the program.

C **Pair work** Exchange your TV review with a partner, and answer these questions.

1. Does your partner's TV review answer all six questions? Find the answers.

2. Is the information in the review organized effectively? How could it be improved?

3. Can you write at least two questions to find out more about the TV program your partner reviewed?

4. Would you like to watch the program your partner wrote about? Why or why not?

Useful expressions

Suggesting improvements
It might be better if you . . .
I think what it needs is . . .
You might want to . . .
It'd be even better if . . .

1 Reading today

starting point

A Read the opinions about reading today. Do you agree with the comments?

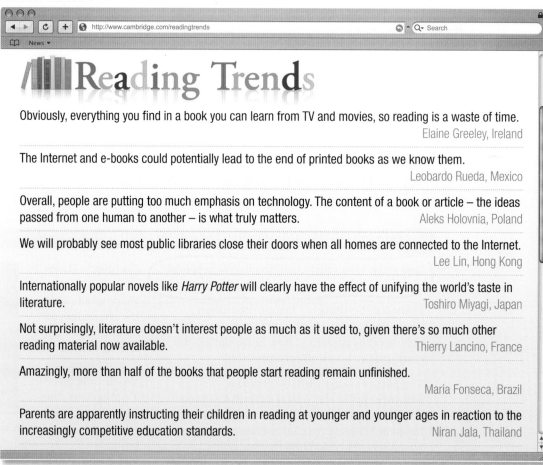

Reading Trends

Obviously, everything you find in a book you can learn from TV and movies, so reading is a waste of time.

Elaine Greeley, Ireland

The Internet and e-books could potentially lead to the end of printed books as we know them.

Leobardo Rueda, Mexico

Overall, people are putting too much emphasis on technology. The content of a book or article – the ideas passed from one human to another – is what truly matters.

Aleks Holovnia, Poland

We will probably see most public libraries close their doors when all homes are connected to the Internet.

Lee Lin, Hong Kong

Internationally popular novels like *Harry Potter* will clearly have the effect of unifying the world's taste in literature.

Toshiro Miyagi, Japan

Not surprisingly, literature doesn't interest people as much as it used to, given there's so much other reading material now available.

Thierry Lancino, France

Amazingly, more than half of the books that people start reading remain unfinished.

Maria Fonseca, Brazil

Parents are apparently instructing their children in reading at younger and younger ages in reaction to the increasingly competitive education standards.

Niran Jala, Thailand

B **Pair work** What role does reading play in your life? Talk about it with a partner.

"Reading is the best way to pass time commuting on the subway. I never go out without a book."

2 Reacting to reading

vocabulary

A Do these adjectives have a positive or a negative meaning? Mark them + or –.

___ a. clichéd   − d. insipid   − g. predictable

+ b. engrossing   + e. inspiring   + h. riveting

___ c. formulaic   + f. moving   + i. touching

B Complete the sentences with one or more of the adjectives above.

1. _____ novels affect your emotions or bring tears to your eyes.

2. A short story is _____ if its plot is obvious and you can guess the ending.

3. A/An __insipid__ article is dull, uninspired, and not worth reading.

4. A/An _____ novel is so full of action you can't put it down.

3 Sentence adverbs

grammar

Sentence adverbs modify a whole sentence, not just part of it. Many adverbs can be used in this way. Sentence adverbs express the speaker's attitude, opinion, or reason for speaking.

Certainty: *clearly, definitely, obviously, unquestionably*
Obviously, everything you find in a book you can learn from TV and movies.

Less certainty: *apparently, evidently, supposedly*
Parents are **apparently** instructing their children in reading at younger and younger ages.

Possibility and probability: *possibly, potentially, probably*
The Internet and e-books could **potentially** lead to the end of printed books as we know them.

Talking honestly and directly: *frankly, honestly, seriously*
Frankly, I'm looking forward to not having to read so much.

Summarizing: *basically, essentially, fundamentally, mainly, overall*
Overall, people are putting too much emphasis on technology.

Other attitudes: *amazingly, surprisingly, not surprisingly, predictably, fortunately, unfortunately*
Not surprisingly, literature doesn't interest people as much as it used to.

Grammar Plus: See page 115.

A Look at the starting point on page 40 again. Can you find the sentence adverb in each person's opinion?

B **Pair work** Rewrite each sentence using one of the adverbs from the grammar box above. Compare with a partner.

1. No one is surprised that many people spend more time online, on the phone, watching TV, and listening to the radio than sleeping.

   Not surprisingly, many people spend more time . . .

2. It's been said that girls read more fiction than boys.

3. It's very likely that movies will replace many forms of literature.

4. In truth, people nowadays rarely read serious literature.

5. It's clear that the Internet will soon beat out all other forms of reading material in all age groups.

6. A potential result is that the Internet could improve people's reading and writing skills.

7. It's amazing that some companies now sell machines that produce single copies of books.

8. It's possible that electronic books will replace paper books sooner than we think.

C **Group work** Use sentence adverbs to express your attitude about trends in the areas below, or use your own ideas. Listen to your classmates' reactions.

- blogs
- television
- online courses
- electronic dictionaries
- magazines
- computer games
- language learning
- notebook computers

"The next generation will probably all have blogs starting in elementary school."
"Yes, that's probably right. Kids are definitely more computer savvy nowadays."

4 The joys of literature

listening

A Pair work In what ways do people benefit from reading literature such as novels, short stories, poetry, and plays? Make a list and share it with the class.

B Listen to Junko (*J*) and Andy (*A*) discuss what people learn from literature. Who introduces the topics in the chart? Write the correct letter.

Topics	Benefits
_J_ 1. practical things	
____ 2. point of view	
____ 3. other countries	
____ 4. writing style	
____ 5. creative writing	
____ 6. escape	

C Listen again. For each topic in the chart above, write at least one benefit you hear. Then share your ideas about the benefits with a partner.

5 Reading choices

discussion

A Pair work Discuss the results of this survey on pleasure-reading preferences. Are women's and men's preferences the same where you live?

Pleasure-Reading Material Preferences for Men and Women in Canada

Men
1. science fiction, fantasy, horror
2. mystery, suspense, spy, detective, adventure
3. history, war, heritage, genealogy
4. science and technology

Women
1. mystery, suspense, spy, detective, adventure
2. romance
3. science fiction, fantasy, horror
4. personal growth

B Group work Which types of reading material in the chart do you personally find the most and least enjoyable? Explain your preferences to the group.

C Group work Brainstorm as many examples of books as you can for the different types of reading genres. Then find out who in your group has read the books, and share your reactions.

"The Lord of the Rings *is an example of fantasy. I've only read one chapter so far. It's riveting!*"

"*Well, I haven't read the books, but fortunately, they are also movies – and I've seen them all.*"

6 Book reviews

reading

A Pair work Have you read any of the books below? Discuss with a partner.

Reviews *from* Readers

One Hundred Years of Solitude
By Gabriel García Márquez

One Hundred Years of Solitude is a book full of colorful characters set in the fictional town of Macondo. The story begins with the romantic dreams of the town's founder, José Arcadio Buendia, and ends with the ruin of his family line and the city he endeavored to make great. It's a riveting book in which so much happens. This moving book will inspire you to connect with your family, love more deeply, dream bigger, and find deeper truths within yourself. Colombian García Márquez was awarded the 1982 Nobel Prize for literature. His book has been translated into more than three dozen languages.

– *Susan Farris, Washington, D.C.*

The Tipping Point
By Malcolm Gladwell

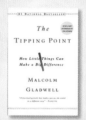

My sister is a marketing major, and she loaned me her favorite book, *The Tipping Point*. At first it seemed pretty technical – I know nothing about marketing – but I finally got the message. Gladwell explains that ideas spread through society much like viruses do. He also claims that certain people are naturally effective communicators who help spread these ideas. And, if the situation is right for an idea to spread, sometimes a small change can then cause it to spread like wildfire. He illustrates his point with convincing examples of successful ideas that have changed the world. If psychology and marketing interest you, I think you'll enjoy *The Tipping Point*.

– *Kate Howson, Manchester, UK*

Tuesdays with Morrie
By Mitch Albom

After discovering his college professor, Morrie, was dying, author Mitch Albom spent fourteen Tuesday afternoons with him learning life's lessons. Clearly, many people have found inspiration in these dying man's last words on aging, family, marriage, and culture, to name a few. It was a best-seller with over a million copies sold. Yet, for those who have done a lot of soul-searching of their own, they might not find self-help books very necessary. Nevertheless, with our busy lives, it is always good to be reminded of the things that are most important in life. Overall, *Tuesdays with Morrie* is a quick read with long-lasting impact.

– *Michael Langdon, San Francisco*

The Harry Potter Series
By J. K. Rowling

The engrossing *Harry Potter* book series really needs no introduction. J. K. Rowling's world of child wizards has captured the imagination of children and adults everywhere. Who isn't attracted to a magical world where photographs can smile, dishes are washed by magic, and where chocolate is good for you? Unfortunately, there is also a dark side. People, even children, die in *Harry Potter* books. Adults lie to children, and life is very often quite unfair. The harassment of children, either by teachers or other students, is another frequent theme. Frankly, I'm not sure that these books would be the right choice for an impressionable child.

– *Gracie Hu, New York*

B Pair work How would these reviewers rate the book they reviewed? Underline language that supports your decision. Share your reasons with your partner.

C Group work Discuss these questions. Then share your answers with the class.

1. Based on the reviews, how likely would you be to read each of the four books?

2. How much would you be influenced by a positive or negative review of a book?

3. What's a book you've read that you'd recommend to others or encourage them to avoid?

1. Taste in music

starting point

A Read the statements expressing different views on music. Which ones do you agree with?

1 I think the more you like to dance, the more you appreciate music with a Latin beat.

2 At first, I didn't like rap music. But the more I listened to the lyrics, the more I understood its powerful social message.

3 Some of the greatest music is in movie soundtracks. The more exciting the soundtrack, the better the movie seems.

4 Radio stations kill music sales by overplaying songs. The more I hear a pop song on the radio, the less I feel like buying it.

5 I'm interested in how a band plays, not how it looks. The more a band focuses on its appearance, the less interesting the music is.

6 Classical music has many layers of complexity. The more knowledgeable you are about it, the more you'll be able to enjoy it.

7 TV commercials often feature a catchy tune – and the catchier the tune, the more likely you are to remember the name of the product.

8 A lot of my friends like to go to clubs with really loud music, but not me. The louder the music gets, the sooner I feel like leaving.

Overheard on the STREETS

B Pair work What kinds of things do you look for in new songs or artists? What makes certain songs more successful than others?

"I love sampling. You know, when artists mix older songs with new music and lyrics."

"Me too. I like recognizable tunes, but with a new twist."

> **Useful expressions**
>
> **Asking about opinions**
> What do you think of/about . . . ?
> How do you feel about . . . ?
> Are you into . . . ?

2. Awesome tunes

listening

A Listen to Adam and Lisa talk about music. What are they doing?

B What are the three types of music Adam and Lisa listen to? What do they think about the types of music they hear? Complete the chart.

Types of music	Lisa's opinions	Adam's opinions

3 Double comparatives

grammar

You can use two comparatives, each preceded by *the*, in order to show how one quality or amount is linked to another. The first comparative expresses a condition for the second comparative.

The more you like to dance, **the more** you appreciate music with a Latin beat.
The more I hear a pop song on the radio, **the less** I feel like buying it.
The more exciting the soundtrack, **the better** the movie seems.
The louder the music gets, **the sooner** I feel like leaving.

Grammar Plus: See page 116.

A Look at the starting point on page 44 again. How many double comparatives can you find?

B **Pair work** Match the clauses to make logical statements. Then compare with a partner. Which statements do you agree with?

1. The more music you try to listen to, __c__
2. The more often you go to dance clubs, ____
3. The more companies a new artist sends a demo CD to, ____
4. The more you study the history of American popular music, ____
5. The less emphasis schools place on music, ____

a. the fewer new musicians will be developed.
b. the more you realize how much influence African music has had on it.
c. the more likely you are to enjoy a wide variety of genres.
d. the greater your chance of suffering some loss of hearing.
e. the better his or her chances are of getting a recording contract.

"I agree with the first statement. Listening to lots of different genres is bound to lead you to appreciate more of them."

C Complete these sentences with your own ideas. Can you add further information to clarify or support the statements you wrote?

1. The earlier children start playing music, . . .
2. The more famous a recording artist becomes, . . .
3. The catchier the melody of a pop song, . . .
4. The more expensive a musical performance is, . . .
5. The more thoughtful the song's lyrics are, . . .
6. The older I get and the more I listen to music, . . .

D **Pair work** Compare and discuss the sentences you wrote above. Share your opinions with the class.

"The earlier children start playing music, the better because music improves memory and increases attention."

"I agree. I think that sometimes we just think of math or language as being beneficial, but in fact, . . ."

4. Describing musical performances

vocabulary

A Look at the collocations below. Match the adjectives used to describe music with their definitions.

1. a **catchy** tune ____
2. a **monotonous** beat ____
3. an **exhilarating** tempo ____
4. **evocative** music ____
5. a **frenetic** pace ____
6. a **haunting** melody ____
7. **mellow** sounds ____
8. a **soothing** rhythm ____

a. fast and energetic, but rather uncontrolled
b. sadly beautiful and difficult to forget
c. making you remember or imagine something pleasant
d. pleasing and easy to remember
e. relaxing, comforting, and removing pain
f. cool, laid-back, and smooth
g. following the same pattern; unchanging
h. making you feel very excited and happy

B **Pair work** Which of the adjectives from above could you use to describe these types of music and performances?

- a live performance by a punk rock band
- the sound of rain and howling wind
- the soundtrack to an action movie
- the sounds of the ocean waves
- fast-paced techno music
- a classical orchestra
- soft jazz with a slow beat
- a children's nursery rhyme

5. Music preferences

discussion

A **Pair work** What kind of music would you expect to hear in these places? What purpose does music serve in each situation?

a gym

a supermarket

a café

B **Group work** What kinds of music do you usually hear in each of these situations? What purposes does the music serve?

1. TV commercials
2. a clothing boutique
3. a doctor's office
4. sports events
5. an elevator
6. movies

C **Group work** What are some of the ways that people use music to enhance their lives at home, at work, or at play?

"I think nowadays music certainly helps lots of people pass the time during a long commute to work."

6. Compare-and-contrast essays

writing

> A compare-and-contrast essay presents the similarities and differences of two or more things. The thesis statement expresses your position on the subject, and it is followed by supporting paragraphs that discuss similarities and differences.

A Read the essay and circle the thesis statement. Then match each paragraph to the headings below. Underline the words that show comparison or contrast.

___ introduction ___ differences ___ conclusion ___ similarities

THE BEATLES VS. the Rolling Stones

❶ Although The Beatles and the Rolling Stones have both been called the "greatest rock-and-roll band of all time," the prize should go to the Rolling Stones. While both bands have had a huge influence on popular music, The Beatles broke up in 1970, and the Rolling Stones are still recording and performing to this day.

❷ Both The Beatles and the Rolling Stones began as four-member British bands that first became popular in the 1960s. The two bands released their first records within a year of each other, and both featured a pair of talented songwriters: Paul McCartney and John Lennon for The Beatles, and Mick Jagger and Keith Richards for the Rolling Stones. Like the Rolling Stones, The Beatles were famous for their cutting-edge style at the time of their debut, and both bands were known for their energetic stage performances.

❸ In the beginning, The Beatles were clean-cut boys with short hair who wore suits. In contrast, the Rolling Stones had a "bad boy" image – they dressed in funky clothes and never smiled. The Beatles' first major hit was the catchy love song "I Want to Hold Your Hand," but the Stones's was a rock song called "Satisfaction." While The Beatles were pop stars, the Rolling Stones were rockers.

❹ It's true that The Beatles did amazing things during the short time they were together, and their innovations are still apparent in today's music. However, the Rolling Stones were the first band to offer the world real rock music. Even in their sixties, the Stones still draw crowds like they did in the 1960s. That says it all.

B Choose two bands, singers, or musical styles to compare and contrast, and make a list of similarities and differences. Then compose a thesis statement that expresses your view.

C Write a four-paragraph essay. Make sure it has an introduction with a clear thesis statement, two paragraphs describing similarities and differences, and an effective conclusion.

D **Pair work** Take turns reading your essays. Do not read your thesis statement. Can your partner guess your point of view?

1. Music success stories

starting point

A Read about these three music success stories. Do you know these singers? Do you know how any other famous singers began their music careers?

Norah Jones

Norah Jones's first musical influence was her mother's extensive music collection. When she was little, she would pick out a disc and play it over and over again. Music was always a part of her life, but it wasn't until she moved to New York that she finally broke into the business.

Usher

In his youth, Usher Raymond would sing each week in his local choir. True talent will always be noticed. He was discovered at age 13 and recorded his first single at age 15. When not recording, the multi-talented star will frequently act on TV, in movies, and in plays.

Christina Aguilera

Even at an early age, Christina Aguilera's rare voice would get people's attention. As a child, she'd dream of being a professional singer. She got her big break in 1992 when she performed on *Star Search*. Later, she made it big with the song "Genie in a Bottle," which topped the charts.

B **Pair work** What qualities and opportunities does a person need to have in order to be a success in the popular music industry? Share your ideas with a partner.

"I think it's important to have an established person in the business take an interest in your talent and help you get your start."

2. Breaking into the business

vocabulary

A Look at these expressions related to show business and fame. Write them in the chart below. Compare with a partner.

be a big hit	be washed up	be a one-hit wonder
be a has-been	get your big break	break into the business
be discovered	make a comeback	make a name for yourself
make it big	pay your dues	get your foot in the door

Just starting out	Currently successful	No longer successful
	be a big hit	

B **Pair work** Talk about famous people you know. How did they start out? Who are still successful? Who are has-beens?

"Mark Wahlberg has really made a name for himself. He went from singer to model to Oscar-nominated actor."

3 *Will* and *would* for habits and general truths

grammar

You can use *would* to express habitual actions in the past. *Would* is more formal than *used to* and is frequently used in past narratives. *Would* needs to be clearly associated with a time in the past.
In his youth, Usher Raymond **would** sing each week in his local choir.

You can use *will* to express personal habits or characteristic behavior in the present.
When not recording, the multi-talented star **will** frequently act on TV, in movies, and in plays.

Will is also used to express facts that are generally true.
True talent **will** always be noticed.

Grammar Plus: See page 117.

A Look at the starting point on page 48 again. Which habitual actions are expressed using *would* and *will*?

B Complete these sentences using the verb in parentheses and *would* or *will*.

1. In my younger days, I __would play__ in a band at local clubs. (play)

2. I love playing the piano. I _____ every chance I get. (practice)

3. After he went deaf, Beethoven _____ music "in his head." (compose)

4 My son doesn't like to practice his guitar. Every time he hears me leave, he _____ practicing until I come back. (stop)

5. When she was only eight years old, Japanese violinist Midori Goto _____ in front of large audiences with confidence. (perform)

6. In high school, British singer-songwriter James Morrison's schoolmates _____ him for playing the guitar instead of playing soccer. (tease)

C Read these descriptions of people. Then use your own ideas to write sentences describing their habitual actions with *would* or *will*.

1. When Ricky was a little boy, he was crazy about his violin.
   He would take it with him wherever he went.

2. Evan is really concerned with world events and listens to the radio every morning.

3. On school trips, we used to pass the time on the bus in various fun ways.

4. When I was younger, the music I listened to was very different from what's on the radio these days.

5. The key to Korean violinist Chin Kim's successful music career is that he teaches and performs.

D **Pair work** Complete these statements with true information. Then write a follow-up sentence using *would* or *will*. Share your answers with a partner.

1. I really enjoy listening to . . .

2. When I was young, I loved . . .

3. It's true that musicians today . . .

"I really enjoy listening to techno music. I'll listen to it when I'm feeling tired or sad, and it will always make me feel better."

4 Guitar blues

A **Pair work** You are going to listen to Marco discussing his music career. What do you think some of his concerns might be? Tell your partner.

B 💿 Now listen to the conversation between Marco and Theresa. What's Marco's biggest problem?

C 💿 Listen again. What advice does Theresa give Marco regarding each of these four areas? Complete the chart.

	Theresa's advice
1. His parents	
2. His opinion of himself	
3. His appearance	
4. The possibility of failure	

5 The secrets of success

A **Group work** Discuss the following questions with your group.

1. What are some of the ways that some actors and singers have made it big?

2. What are some of the things that successful people have in common?

3. What is your definition of *success*?

B Read the advice for success below. Check (✓) the three pieces of advice that you think are most useful.

★★ Advice for Success ★★

○ **1. Don't be afraid to dream.** You don't need to accept limitations others put on you.

○ **2. Don't talk about your plans too much.** Spend that energy making things happen.

○ **3. Take yourself seriously.** Pursue your dreams with conviction.

○ **4. Don't try to do it all alone.** Seek out the people and resources you need.

○ **5. Always appear confident** – even if you don't always feel that way inside.

○ **6. Think positively.** Don't let yourself think negative thoughts for very long.

○ **7. Don't be afraid to fail.** All successful people will fail – and learn a lot from it.

○ **8. Dress for success.** Figure out how you need to look to get what you want.

C **Group work** Tell the group which three pieces of advice you chose. Explain why you think they are useful for you.

6. Subwaymusicians

A **Pair work** Are there street musicians in your city? What do you think of them? Discuss with a partner. Then read the article.

Making Music Under the Streets of New York

Straining to make his music heard over the roar of trains and the traffic-clogged streets of Manhattan, singer-songwriter Theo Eastwind is far away from the bright lights of the big-time music industry. That's just fine with him. "I'm not in this for big money. I'm just making a living," Eastwind said between songs.

Eastwind is one of more than 100 official subway musicians performing throughout the 468-station New York subway system. Scores of other musicians perform unofficially. Although musicians have been playing the New York subway system for decades, a transit-sponsored program was established in 1987 to spruce up the city's subway stations. Each spring, a panel of judges determines which performers are accepted into the program. "This gives them a way to be organized, and it gives them a space to play so that they're not fighting for a little corner," a spokeswoman said. For many tourists in the Big Apple, however, subway musicians add local color to what can be a frustrating attempt to navigate the city's complex transit system. For New Yorkers, live tunes can make their stuffy commutes a little more pleasant.

Eastwind, who came to New York from Austria a decade ago, now regularly plays throughout the subway system, on the street, and in local clubs. With a well-worn T-shirt and light hair peaking out from beneath a cap, he looks – and acts – the part of a street musician perfectly. On a recent afternoon, his open guitar case collecting money in front of him, Eastwind contemplated his role as a musician. "Underground musicians, or street musicians, are a continuation of the culture of troubadours, early singer-songwriters in Europe," he said. However, musicians playing to the three million daily commuters on New York's subway face a special set of challenges.

"Playing in the subways is difficult because you have people who don't come down here to see you; they just want to catch the train," Eastwind said. "So you've got a window of maybe ten to twenty seconds to get their interest and, if there's no train, to keep their interest. You've got to mold yourself to what people like."

Source: "Striving to Make Music Under the Streets of NYC," by Danel Strieff and Jon Sweeney, MSNBC

B Read the article again. Are these statements true (*T*), false (*F*), or is the answer not given (*NG*)? Correct the false statements to make them true.

____ 1. New York has been licensing street musicians for decades.

____ 2. The sole purpose of New York's underground music program is to regulate musicians.

____ 3. Theo Eastwind had to pass an audition to become an official underground musician.

____ 4. Eastwind has no ambition to become a part of the mainstream music industry.

____ 5. Eastwind considers himself to be similar to the troubadours.

____ 6. According to Eastwind, playing underground is the same as playing in clubs.

C **Group work** Discuss these questions. Then share your answers with the class.

1. Do you think New York City's system of licensing official underground musicians would work where you are? Why or why not?

2. Have you ever given money to a street or subway performer? Why or why not?

Communication review

Self-assessment

How well can you do these things? Rate your ability from 1 to 5 (1 = low, 5 = high).

Discuss television shows using adjectives and sentence adverbs (Ex. 1)	_____
Recommend books using *such . . . that* and *so . . . that* (Ex. 2)	_____
Listen to a radio program using sentence adverbs and *will* for habits (Ex. 3)	_____
Give opinions about music and songs using double comparatives (Ex. 4)	_____

Now do the corresponding exercises below. Were your ratings correct?

 My kind of show

discussion

A Think of an example of each type of television show. For each show, write at least one good point about it and one change that would improve it.

Type of show	Example	Good points	Changes you'd make
game show			
documentary			
reality TV			
soap opera			
talk show			
drama series			

B Pair work Compare your ideas with a partner. Use sentence adverbs.

"I really like House, M.D. – it's so engrossing."

"Me too. Apparently they have a big team of researchers. I guess that's why it's so convincing."

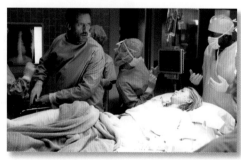

 You have to read this!

discussion

A Talk about your reading habits. Give an example for each of these topics.

1. a book you would recommend
2. the most interesting character you've ever come across in a story
3. a book you would like to see made or was already made into a movie
4. a magazine, newspaper, website, or blog you read regularly

B Pair work Discuss your ideas with a partner.

"I recommend Thirteen Moons. It was so interesting that I couldn't put it down."

3. Superstitious actors

listening

A You are going to listen to a radio show about superstitions in the acting profession. Why do you think actors might be more superstitious than nonactors?

B Now listen to the program. What is the main reason Jeffrey gives for increased superstition among actors? Check (✓) the correct answer.

  ☐ a. They feel isolated from the rest of society.

  ☐ b. They are insecure.

  ☐ c. They travel a lot.

C Listen again. Check (✓) the theater superstition you hear in each pair.

1. ☐ a. Black cats are considered lucky.

   ☐ b. Black cats are considered unlucky.

2. ☐ a. It is unlucky for a cat to sleep on a costume.

   ☐ b. It is good luck when a cat falls asleep on a costume.

3. ☐ a. The number 13 is believed to be lucky.

   ☐ b. The number 13 is believed to be unlucky.

4. ☐ a. It is unlucky to act in the play *Macbeth*.

   ☐ b. It is unlucky to say the name of the play *Macbeth*.

4. Hit songs

speaking

A **Pair work** What are the five best songs from the last three years? Make a list of five songs you both agree on.

B **Group work** Join another pair and try to agree on a list of three songs. Then share your list with the rest of the class. Is there one song that appears on all the lists?

"How do you feel about . . . ?"

"Well, the more I hear it, the more I like it. But I'm not sure it's one of the best songs from the last three years. What do you think about . . . ?"

Changing times

1 How we are changing

starting point

A People's lifestyles are changing more quickly than ever before. Have you noticed any of these trends in your community?

ORGANIC PRODUCE

Lifestyle Trends

1 A growing number of people who are concerned with the effect of pesticides on the environment are buying organic produce.

2 Hybrid cars – cars powered by both gas and electricity – are an option that more people are choosing in order to save money and reduce pollution.

3 More professionals whose managers allow it are opting to "telecommute," or work from home.

4 There is a wider variety of vitamins that health-conscious customers want.

5 Alternative therapies that help fight stress, such as massage, are on the rise.

6 Vegetarianism is a growing trend among people who feel it is unhealthy or simply wrong to eat animal products.

7 These days, a person whose body isn't perfect (and whose is?) is more likely to resort to cosmetic surgery.

8 Coffee shops are everywhere, charging higher and higher prices to the caffeine-addicted customers who they serve.

B **Pair work** Discuss the good points and bad points of each trend. Which do you think are the most beneficial?

"Organic produce is so much better for the environment and your health."

"I guess so, but organic fruit and vegetables are so expensive."

2 Current trends

discussion

A Think of a current trend in your country, community, or among people you know for as many of these areas as you can.

- education
- the environment
- family
- food
- health
- housing
- technology
- travel

B **Group work** Share your ideas with the group. Discuss them, and decide on the three most significant trends. Report them to the class and explain why they are significant.

"One trend we discussed is that people are really into eco-tourism. This move toward environmentally friendly travel is significant because . . . "

3 Optional and required relative pronouns

grammar

In defining relative clauses, when the relative pronoun is the subject of the clause or it shows possession, the relative pronoun is required. When it is the object, it is usually optional.

Subject of clause (relative pronouns *that*, *which*, or *who* required)
People **who** / **that** are concerned with the effect of pesticides on the environment are buying organic produce.
Alternative therapies **that** / **which** help fight stress are on the rise.

Showing possession (relative pronoun *whose* required)
More professionals **whose** managers allow it are opting to "telecommute," or work from home.

Object of clause (relative pronouns *that*, *which*, *who*, or *whom* optional)
Hybrid cars are an option (**that** / **which**) more people are choosing.
Coffee shops are everywhere, charging higher and higher prices to the caffeine-addicted customers (**who** / **whom** / **that**) they serve.

Grammar Plus: See page 118.

A Look at the starting point on page 54 again. In which sentences is the relative pronoun required?

B Check (✓) the sentences in which the relative pronoun is optional. How many sentences are true for your community?

☐ 1. Young families who dream of owning a house are finding they can't afford one.

☐ 2. The pressure that students feel to succeed in school is increasing.

☐ 3. People who used to go to theaters to watch movies now watch them at home on DVD.

☐ 4. Fishermen now travel long distances to find fish that they used to catch locally.

☐ 5. The new generation of young politicians tends to keep the promises that they make.

☐ 6. People are devoting more time to others who are less fortunate.

☐ 7. People are recycling many things which they would have thrown away in the past.

☐ 8. A lot of people who have grown tired of city life are moving to the country.

C Is the relative pronoun in these sentences the subject of the clause (*S*), the object of the clause (*O*), or does it show possession (*P*)? Write the correct letter.

____ 1. Is the number of young people **who** opt for cosmetic surgery growing or shrinking?

____ 2. Is it harmful for children **whose** parents both work to be sent to day care?

____ 3. Are genetically modified crops an option **that** farmers are considering?

____ 4. Are the problems **that** arise nowadays between couples different from those in the past?

____ 5. Are there any alternative therapies **that** you think are ineffective or even dangerous?

____ 6. Is it becoming more difficult for people **who** do not speak English fluently to get a job?

D Pair work Interview each other using the questions above.

4. Antonyms with prefixes

vocabulary & speaking

A The antonyms of these adjectives can be formed by adding the prefix *il-*, *im-*, *in-*, or *ir-*. Write the correct prefix in front of each adjective.

a. ___considerate   c. ___decisive   e. ___mature   g. ___responsible

b. ___consistent   d. ___logical   f. ___proper   h. ___tolerant

B Now complete the opinions with one of the antonyms above. Write the correct letter.

1. "You can be 40 and still be ___ if you refuse to grow up and have the expected behavior for a person your age."

2. "People today just don't care about following correct rules or manners. They have such ___ behavior."

3. "Today's politicians are so ___ . They just change their opinions and statements from one day to the next."

4. "Selfish people are often ___ of others and don't care about their feelings."

5. "___ people refuse to accept ideas and behavior different from their own."

6. "Many accidents happen when people are ___ and don't give careful thought to the result of their actions."

7. "Because young people lack wisdom and reason, they often make ___ decisions."

8. "Many young people are ___ about their future and unable to choose a course of action."

C **Pair work** Do you agree with the opinions above? Discuss with a partner.

5. Generation gap

listening

A Listen to Chris and Paula talk about the differences between their generation and their parents' during this on-the-street interview. In their opinion, what is different? Write the changes in the chart below.

B Listen again. Do Chris and Paula feel that the changes are positive (*P*) or negative (*N*)? Write the correct letter in the chart. Do you agree?

Areas	Change	Positive or negative?
career and family		
expectations about material things		
acceptance of others		

6. Writing about a personal experience

writing

A personal-experience composition usually begins with an introductory paragraph containing a thesis statement and some observations or comments. The body of the composition provides background information and gives details about what happened. The conclusion usually restates the thesis and presents the writer's feelings.

A Underline the thesis statement. Then read the composition and answer the questions below. Compare answers with a partner.

Last month I took a giant step and finally moved to a new apartment. I had been sharing a two-bedroom apartment for two years with a friend who I'd known since childhood, and decided that it was time to have my own place. In the beginning, I was a little scared because I would be assuming a great deal of financial responsibility. I was also a little concerned about feeling lonely, but I knew it was important to have the experience of being totally on my own.

The first thing I wanted to do before making a final decision was to talk things over with my roommate. We had first moved in together because neither of us could afford . . .

I looked at many apartments before making up my mind. I finally found one that I liked – an affordable one-bedroom in very good shape, with a lot of light. The apartment is . . .

My apartment now is beginning to look like a home. I've been looking at a lot of interior design websites, and I've managed to decorate my apartment. . . .

Looking back, I definitely think that I made the right decision. I feel really good about having a place I can call my own. I feel more independent and responsible. Sometimes I still feel a little lonely, but for the most part, I enjoy the privacy.

1. What observations or personal comments does the writer make in the first paragraph?

2. What kinds of details and background information does the body of the composition provide?

3. What additional information do you think the writer gives to complete the paragraphs?

B Write a composition about something that has happened to you recently. Make sure to include an introductory paragraph, three paragraphs with details, and a conclusion.

C **Pair work** Exchange papers and answer these questions.

1. Does your partner's introductory paragraph have a thesis statement?

2. Do all the details in the body of the composition support the thesis statement?

3. What other points or examples could be added?

1 Human treasures

starting point

A Read about these people who preserve ancient artistic traditions. Which of these traditional arts have you seen?

Hamish Moore is a well-known maker of bagpipes in Scotland. He makes them just the way craftsmen did centuries ago. Listening to Hamish play his pipes can make you feel as if you've been transported back in time.

Pualani Kanaka'ole Kanahele is a famous scholar and a teacher of hula, a traditional dance in Hawaii. She feels as though hula is a gift from her Polynesian ancestors. It's her joy and responsibility to continue the tradition.

In 2005, **Hara Kiyoshi** of Japan was designated a "living national treasure" for his pottery. As his great teachers did before him, he uses age-old techniques, but produces contemporary pieces known for their beautiful motifs.

B Pair work Look at these categories. For how many of them can you think of an ancient tradition that continues in the present day?

- clothing
- dance
- literature
- painting
- cooking
- drama
- music
- transportation

C Group work Share some of your ideas of ancient traditions with your classmates. Discuss why you think it is important to preserve them. How can they be preserved?

"I think it's important to preserve the Yaqui Indian 'Dance of the Deer.' It has been performed in Mexico since before the Spanish came. It's such a beautiful dance!"

2 Lost memories

listening

A Listen to Kent and Julia talk about how long photos and movies last. What is the problem with what Julia is doing?

B Listen again. About how long can each of the following be expected to last? Complete the chart.

	About how long do they last?
photographs	
CDs	
magnetic tape	
normal film	

3 As if, as though, as, the way, and like

grammar

As if and *as though* often introduce clauses that describe impressions about feelings or behavior after verbs such as *act*, *behave*, *feel*, *look*, *seem*, and *talk*.
She feels **as if / as though** hula is a gift from her Polynesian ancestors.

As and *the way* introduce clauses that express a comparison.
He makes them just **as / the way** craftsmen did centuries ago.

In informal English, the word *like* can be substituted for *as if / as though* and *as / the way*.
As his great teachers did before him, he uses age-old techniques.
Like his great teachers did before him, he uses age-old techniques.

Grammar Plus: See page 119.

A Look at the starting point on page 58 again. Can you find another expression you can rewrite with *like*?

B Rewrite these sentences to make them more formal using *as if, as though, as,* or *the way.* Compare your answers with a partner.

1. Lately, I'm trying to use the telephone more, like I did before I got e-mail.

   Lately, I'm trying to use the telephone more, the way I did before I got e-mail.

2. These days, women are not expected to stay at home like their mothers did.

3. Sometimes I feel like the world is changing too fast.

4. I have a friend who studies Latin like she's going to need it to communicate someday.

5. There are people in the Amazon who live like time has stood still for a thousand years.

6. Nobody in my family cooks like my grandmother did, since no one saved her recipes.

C **Pair work** Complete these sentences so that they are true for you. Add another sentence with your own information, and compare with a partner.

1. Young people today still act as though . . .

   they have no worries.

2. I don't feel the need to . . . as so many people do these days.

3. I feel as though I never have enough time to . . .

4. I wish I could still . . . the way I used to when I was younger.

5. My family still . . . , just as my grandparents used to do.

6. _____

D **Group work** Join another pair and share your answers. Ask for more specific information, and give your opinions.

"*I really feel as if the older generation is too critical of young people.*"
"*What makes you say that?*"
"*Well, I think they need to remember how difficult life can be for us.*"

Useful expressions

Asking for more specific information
What makes you say that?
Why do you think that?
In what way(s)?

4 Collocations with *change*

A Look at the expressions with *change*. Match each expression with its definition.

1. advocate ____	
2. block ____	
3. cope with ____	
4. facilitate ____	(a) change
5. initiate ____	
6. resist ____	
7. welcome ____	

a. stop a change from happening

b. start a change

c. successfully deal with a change

d. fight against a change

e. make a change happen more easily

f. speak in favor of a change

g. invite a change and be happy about it

B Pair work Use the expressions with *change* to tell your partner how you would react to these situations. Then discuss your reactions.

1. a four-day workweek
2. stricter traffic law enforcement
3. laws restricting pet ownership
4. eliminating fast-food restaurants

"I would advocate a change for stricter traffic laws. I think there are too many dangerous drivers on the roads today."

5 How do you cope?

A Complete the survey. How true is each statement for you? Circle 1 to 5. Then discuss the survey with a partner.

DO YOU RESIST OR WELCOME CHANGE?	Not true at all				Very true
1. I set realistic goals for myself and take steps to achieve them.	1	2	3	4	5
2. I am a curious person and enjoy new experiences.	1	2	3	4	5
3. I live in the present, appreciate the past, and focus on the future.	1	2	3	4	5
4. I listen to others and seek understanding.	1	2	3	4	5
5. When solving a problem, I seek advice and support from friends and family I trust.	1	2	3	4	5
6. I am highly flexible and easygoing.	1	2	3	4	5
7. I am creative and brainstorm solutions to challenges.	1	2	3	4	5
8. I stand up for myself and say "no" when I need to.	1	2	3	4	5
9. When I fail at something, I see it as a learning experience.	1	2	3	4	5
10. I try to find humor in all situations.	1	2	3	4	5

SCORE

10–20 You tend to block change. You need to learn to better facilitate change in your life.

21–30 You're somewhat resistant to change. Friends and family can help you cope with it.

31–40 You basically welcome change. However, there is always room for improvement.

41–50 You are exceptionally adaptable. You initiate positive changes in your life.

B Pair work Think of a big change in your life. Tell your partner what happened.

"Getting my driver's license was a welcome change. I could finally go where I wanted when I wanted . . ."

6 Return to simplicity

reading

A **Pair work** Would you reduce your income by half in exchange for more free time and less stress? Discuss with a partner. Then read the article.

Leaving the Rat Race for the Simple Life

Time is more precious than money for an increasing number of people who are choosing to live more with less – and welcome the change.

Kay and Charles Giddens, a paralegal and a trial lawyer, respectively, sold their home to start a bed and breakfast. Four years later, the couple dishes out banana pancake breakfasts, cleans toilets, serves homemade chocolate chip cookies to guests in a bed and breakfast surrounded by trees on a mesa known for colorful sunsets.

"Do I miss the freeways? Do I miss the traffic? Do I miss the stress? No," says Ms. Giddens. "This is a phenomenon that's fairly widespread. A lot of people are reevaluating their lives and figuring out what they want to do.

Simple living ranges from cutting down on weeknight activities to sharing housing, living closer to work and commuting less, avoiding shopping malls, borrowing books from the library instead of buying them, and taking a cut in pay to work at a more pleasurable job.

Vicki Robin, a writer, tells us how she copes with the changes in her budget, now just a fifth of what she used to make.

"You become conscious about where your money is going and how valuable it is," Ms. Robin says. "You tend not to use things up. You cook at home rather than eat out. Your life is less frantic, and you discover your expenses have gone way down. People are very interested in how they can simplify their lives, save money, and get out of debt."

Janet Luhrs, a lawyer, quit her practice after giving birth and leaving her daughter with a nanny for two weeks. "It was not the way I wanted to raise my kids," she says. "Simplicity is not just about saving money, it's about me sitting down every night with my kids to a candlelit dinner with classical music."

Mrs. Luhrs now edits an online newsletter, *Simple Living*, which publishes tips on how to buy recycled furniture and shoes, organize potluck dinners instead of fancy receptions, and advocates changes in consumption patterns.

"It's not about poverty or deprivation," Mrs. Luhrs explains. "It's about conscious living and creating the life you want. The less stuff you buy, the less money goes out the door, and the less money you have to earn."

Source: "More People Are Leaving the Rat Race for the Simple Life," by Julia Duin, *The Washington Times*

B Complete the summary of the article. Fill in each blank with no more than three words from the article.

Many people have come to think that time is (1) _____ than money. The Giddenses gave up their law careers to run a (2) _____ , and they are happy they did. Others have chosen to (3) _____ their lives by, for example, sharing housing or cutting expenses. Janet Luhrs quit her job as a lawyer to spend more time with (4) _____ . She now edits a (5) _____ called *Simple Living*. She understands that the less stuff you (6) _____ , the less (7) _____ you need to earn.

C **Group work** Discuss these questions. Then share your answers with the class.

1. Do you think the people in the article have improved their lives? Why?

2. What changes would you make to live more simply?

LESSON A · What's new on the market?

1. Smart shoppers

starting point

A **Pair work** Read these statements about ways to find bargains. Which ones have you or your partner tried?

$MART $HOPPERS How do you find the best bargains?

"I recently discovered online auctions. Members sell each other all kinds of stuff. I really get excited about the bidding — sometimes there's lots of competition. But sometimes you're the only bidder. See this hat? It only cost me two dollars!" **Rick, 24**

"Before I shop, I always look in the newspaper to find out about any sales going on, and I always check my mail and e-mail for information about sales — many stores mail customers fliers about sales, or they'll announce a big sale to customers by e-mail." **Jacinda, 32**

"Do you get tired of clothes quickly? Do you always want to buy yourself something new? Let me give you a tip. I buy secondhand clothes at thrift shops. I can always find something I like — even designer brands — at a greatly reduced price!" **Norma, 21**

"For food and everyday items, I recommend wholesale clubs to everyone I know. For a small membership fee, you can go to a big warehouselike store that sells everything in bulk – in large quantities. The rule there is "the more you buy, the more you save."" **Ling-wei, 43**

B **Pair work** What other ways do you find bargains? Can you remember an item you bought at a reduced price?

"There are some great discount stores downtown that sell electronics, and you can find some awesome bargains. I got a great digital camera there for half price."

2. Shopping preferences

listening

A Listen to Ben and Anna talk about their shopping preferences. Where do they like to shop?

1. Ben: _____   2. Anna: _____

B Listen again. Write three reasons they give for their preferences in the chart.

Ben's reasons	Anna's reasons

C **Pair work** Do you prefer traditional or Internet shopping? Explain your reasons.

3 Placement of direct and indirect objects

grammar

For most verbs in English, including *give, lend, mail, offer, sell, send, show, teach,* and *tell,* direct and indirect objects follow these patterns:

Pattern A
direct object + *to* + indirect object
Stores mail **fliers to customers**.
Stores mail **fliers to them**.
Stores mail **them to customers**.
Stores mail **them to them**.

Pattern B
indirect object + direct object
Stores mail **customers fliers**.
Stores mail **them fliers**.

With verbs such as *announce, describe, explain, mention, provide, recommend, return,* and *say,* the indirect object cannot precede the direct object. Sentences follow Pattern A above.
They'll announce **a big sale (it) to customers (them)** by e-mail.

With verbs such as *allow, ask, cause,* and *cost,* the indirect object precedes the direct object and takes no preposition. Sentences follow Pattern B above.
It only cost **Rick two dollars**!
It only cost **me two dollars**!

Grammar Plus: See page 120.

A Look at the starting point on page 62 again. Find sentences containing both a direct and an indirect object. Which pattern do they follow?

B Complete these sentences using the words in parentheses. Whenever possible, write the sentence in two different ways.

1. Many companies use cartoon characters to sell . . . (products / children)

   products to children. / children products.

2. If I'm not satisfied with a product, I never hesitate to return . . . (it / the store)

3. The Internet has made shopping much easier, but delivery costs . . . (more money / people)

4. Good salespeople are able to convincingly explain . . . (the benefits of a product / their customers)

5. At discount stores, when they lower prices, they always announce . . . (it / the shoppers)

6. When I told the baker the bread smelled good, he gave . . . (a free sample / me)

7. In most malls, there is a mall directory that shows . . . (the locations of all the stores / customers)

8. At restaurants, my wife thinks I ask (too many questions / the waiter)

C **Pair work** Use the verbs below to talk about things you've bought recently. Ask follow-up questions.

ask	describe	give	return
cost	explain	recommend	tell

"A friend recommended a new discount store to me, and I finally went there last weekend."
"What kinds of things do they sell?"
"Mainly high-tech electronics and stuff like that."
"Did you buy anything?"
"Yeah. I bought a flat screen TV."

Shopping experiences

vocabulary & speaking

A Pair work Match each expression with its meaning. Then compare with a partner.

1. go over your credit limit _g_
2. be a bargain hunter ____
3. be a compulsive shopper ____
4. have buyer's remorse ____
5. make an impulse buy ____
6. bid on an item ____
7. go on a shopping spree ____
8. go window-shopping ____

a. have regrets after making an unwise purchase
b. be unable to control your need to buy things
c. buy something suddenly without having planned to
d. spend lots of money shopping for pleasure
e. enjoy looking at goods in stores without buying any
f. be a person who looks for low-priced products
g. charge more to your credit card than the allowed amount
h. compete against others to buy an item at an auction

B Group work Which of these experiences related to shopping have you had? Share your experiences with the group. Use the expressions above where appropriate.

- You bought something and later wished you hadn't.
- You resisted buying something you wanted.
- You were inspired by an advertisement to buy something.

"I made an impulse buy and got an expensive hat, and now it just hangs in my closet."

Are you a compulsive shopper?

discussion

A Pair work Which statements are true for you? Check (✔) *yes* or *no* for each statement. Then discuss your answers with a partner.

What Are Your SHOPPING HABITS?	Yes	No
1. I can never go shopping without making an impulse buy.	☐	☐
2. I often buy things that I end up never wearing or using.	☐	☐
3. At home, I frequently feel tempted to go online and buy something.	☐	☐
4. When I visit a new city, I spend most of my free time shopping.	☐	☐
5. I always feel guilty after going on a shopping spree.	☐	☐
6. I have gone over my credit limit at least once.	☐	☐
7. As soon as new fashions appear in the stores, I have to buy them.	☐	☐
8. After buying things, I sometimes lie to relatives and friends about the price.	☐	☐
9. I sometimes go shopping to forget my troubles.	☐	☐

B Group work Discuss these questions and share your ideas with the class.

1. What are some other characteristics of a compulsive shopper?
2. What other problems do compulsive shoppers face?
3. What would you do to help a compulsive shopper?

6 Supporting an opinion

writing

> When writing a composition that supports an opinion, first present the opinion in the thesis statement. Then support it in subsequent paragraphs with examples and details.

A Read the composition and discuss the questions.

1. What is the writer's opinion?
2. What are the reasons given to support the opinion?

Because credit cards present many advantages, they have become widespread. However, the use of credit cards also causes problems. With unlimited credit, people spend too much money. I think there should be a limit to the amount of credit people can have. This way, the total amount of credit on all of their credit cards together could never go over a certain percentage of their income.

Many compulsive shoppers run up such high debts that they go bankrupt, creating problems for their families as well as for the people to whom they owe money. Currently, it is easy for people to accumulate many credit cards. Although the credit cards have limits, the number of credit cards is not limited. People with ten credit cards, each with a $5,000 limit, have $50,000 of credit, even though they might not be able to pay all of their bills. Such a situation can quickly lead to bankruptcy.

People need to be given an absolute credit limit. If people were not permitted to go over this limit, they would have to be more responsible with their money and evaluate which purchases were most important to them. I think that the actual limit on credit card spending should be based on income so that credit would be based on the ability to pay.

B Complete one of these opinions on shopping or use one of your own. Then present your opinion in a thesis statement.

1. No one under 21 should be allowed to . . .
2. People with a lot of debt should . . .
3. Stores should never give cash refunds for . . .
4. Customers who break an item in a store should . . .
5. Shoplifters should do community service by . . .

C Make a list of details or examples to support your thesis statement. Then write a composition with an introductory paragraph containing your opinion, and at least one paragraph with supporting examples or details.

D **Pair work** Take turns reading each other's compositions. Can you think of additional examples or details your partner could use to be more persuasive?

1 Print advertisements

starting point

A **Pair work** Look at the three advertisements. Which kind do you think is the most effective? Where else do you see advertisements?

magazine ads   *company logos*   *billboards*

B **Pair work** Read these opinions about advertisements. Do you agree with them? What do you think makes a good advertisement?

- "I think consumers need to insist that advertisements be truthful in every respect."

- "It seems to me that a good ad is a memorable ad – one that sticks in your head."

- "I believe it is essential that an ad be clever and witty in order to be effective."

- "Some ads seem to demand that the customer buy the product. I don't like a 'hard sell' approach."

- "I think it's crucial that an ad clearly communicate the benefits of the product it is selling."

2 Radio ads

listening

A **Pair work** What types of products or services are typically advertised on the radio? Do you think radio is an effective advertising medium?

B Listen to three radio advertisements. What products are they for? Write the name and type of each product in the chart below.

C Listen again. What benefits of the products are highlighted in the ads? Complete the chart.

Name of product	Type of product	Benefit(s)
1.		
2.		
3.		

3 Verbs in the subjunctive

grammar

Certain expressions and verbs such as *demand*, *insist*, *propose*, *recommend*, *request*, and *suggest* are followed by the subjunctive. The subjunctive uses the base form of the verb. It is generally used in formal language to express a wish or necessity.

I think consumers need to insist (that) **advertisements be** truthful in every respect.
Some ads seem to demand (that) **the customer buy** the product.

These expressions are frequently followed by the subjunctive:

it is crucial   it is imperative   it is important
it is essential   it is vital   it is critical

I believe it is essential that **an ad be** clever and witty in order to be effective.

Grammar Plus: See page 121.

A Look at the starting point on page 66 again. Which opinion does not use the subjunctive?

B Use verbs followed by the subjunctive instead of *should* or *must* to complete these sentences without changing the meaning.

1. Companies should increase advertising budgets to increase sales. (I / suggest)

   I suggest that companies increase advertising budgets to increase sales.

2. All ad agencies should use humor in their ads. (It is important)

3. Cities should tear down billboards that obstruct city views. (I / demand)

4. The government must regulate ads on the Internet. (It is essential)

5. Everyone should buy a digital video recorder that skips commercials. (I / recommend)

6. Industries selling harmful products must be stopped from advertising. (It is crucial)

C **Group work** Use these verbs and expressions to give the people below advice on their problems with advertising. Do you ever have similar problems? Ask your group for advice.

insist	it is crucial	it is essential
propose	recommend	suggest

Useful expressions

Asking for advice
What do you think I should do?
What would you do if you were me?
What would you do if you were in my position?

❶ "The fast food in commercials and posters always looks great. It looks so good I can't resist buying some, but what they actually give me looks pretty bad and really unappetizing."

❷ "I saw a clothing store with a big 'Going Out of Business' sign in the window last year, so I went in and bought a lot of clothes. Now, it's a year later, and the sign is still there."

❸ "I got an interesting e-mail message last week, the subject of which was 'You're a winner!' Well, I opened it, and now my computer doesn't work anymore."

4 Marketing strategies

vocabulary

A These expressions are used to describe marketing strategies. Write the correct letter to complete the sentences below.

a. a free sample   d. telemarketing   g. a frequent buyer program

b. e-mail spam   e. behavioral targeting   h. an online TV commercial

c. product placement   f. a celebrity endorsement

___ 1. allows products to be placed in movies or on TV shows

___ 2. links the names and images of famous people to products

___ 3. lets people try a product they weren't planning on buying

___ 4. involves tracking customers' Web surfing habits in order to market to them what they want

___ 5. encourages loyalty by rewarding customers who shop a lot

___ 6. often precedes Internet news or clips so viewers are forced to watch them

___ 7. sneaks through most Internet security software with unwanted offers

___ 8. allows salespeople to speak individually with potential customers over a wide area

B **Pair work** Do any of the expressions above describe undercover marketing strategies, in which people are not aware that they are being marketed to?

5 The ethics of undercover marketing

discussion

A **Pair work** How would you feel if you thought someone was being friendly to you, but was secretly trying to sell you something? Discuss your feelings with your partner.

B **Group work** Read about undercover marketing, and discuss the questions below with your group.

> **Undercover marketers** (also called stealth marketers) try to find ways to introduce products to people without actually letting them know that they are being marketed to. Here are three actual techniques that have been used for undercover marketing.
>
> | | | |
> |---|---|---|
> | The product is a video gaming glove that allows gamers to control games with small finger movements. Unknown actors go into coffee shops and enthusiastically use the glove. This attracts interested people. The actor lets them try it out, never saying who he is. | A top camera phone company sent 60 actors to ten cities with their latest model. The actors pretended to be tourists, and asked people to take their picture. In this way, they put the new phone in people's hands and taught them how to use it. | To promote a newly released animated movie, a staff including teenagers as young as 13 went to Internet chat rooms, blogs, and message boards and posted positive reviews for the movie. The staff kept their true identity secret. |

1. Which of these three marketing techniques seems the most unethical to you? Why?

2. Do you think undercover marketing should be controlled by the government? Why or why not?

6 Stealth advertising

reading

A **Pair work** Do you think consumers are more likely to take notice of an unusual advertising gimmick than they would a traditional TV commercial? Discuss with a partner. Then read the article to compare your ideas with the author's.

Guerrillas IN OUR MIDST

As consumers lose interest in traditional advertising, "guerrilla" marketing, which relies on eye-catching stunts, is becoming fashionable. But much of it misses the mark. Even by New York standards, things have been odd on the streets lately. Some 8,000 wallets were dropped onto Manhattan's pavements last winter, but not by careless shoppers. Instead of cash inside, curious New Yorkers found a card and the address of a charity website, at which they could donate money. More recently an Internet search engine sent 35 actors dressed as British butlers to the U.S. Open tennis tournament to guide visitors to their seats and answer tennis trivia questions. Established firms are acting oddly, too. This summer, a chain restaurant helped to bankroll Russia's space agency by putting a ten-meter-high, $1.25 million ad on a booster rocket launched into space. In America, marketers have even approached a soft drink company with the idea of projecting its logo onto the moon.

Marketing gimmicks are hardly new, but they are becoming more frequent, more extreme, and more ubiquitous – earning a label all of their own: *guerrilla marketing.* One advantage of guerrilla marketing, claim its fans, is that it is cheaper than typical TV or print advertising. This has particular appeal to Internet firms as they run out of cash, having poured too much money into traditional advertising. A health-advice site cut its monthly marketing budget by 95%, to $50,000, by reducing paid TV advertising. Instead, it relies on buzz from marketing stunts, such as giving away free products.

Of course, guerrilla marketing's appeal is often superficial. A quick Internet search throws out 12,000 references to the term, but most of the websites are surprisingly ordinary. Many stunts are neither memorable nor big enough to raise brand awareness and boost sales.

While there is no doubt that extreme marketing can create buzz, raising false expectations lays advertisers open to criticism, especially if the products they push end up being nothing special. Good marketing simply helps word-of-mouth to spread. If advertisers are smart, guerrilla marketing could evolve into something that is as focused as it is fun. If not, it will do little but add to the noise.

Source: "The Rise of 'Guerilla' Marketing," The Economist

B **Pair work** In your own words, take turns explaining how each of these companies conducted their guerrilla marketing. What do you think of each of the ideas?

1. the charity website
2. the search engine
3. the chain restaurant
4. the soft drink company
5. the health-advice site

C **Group work** Discuss these questions. Then share your answers with the class.

1. Which of the examples of guerrilla marketing mentioned in the article would be most and least effective where you are? Explain.

2. Why might some guerrilla marketing efforts backfire or raise false expectations? Give examples from the article and your own experience.

3. Choose a product and plan a guerrilla marketing gimmick to promote it in your country.

LESSON A · Animals in our lives

1 Amazing animals

starting point

A Read about these three famous animals. Have you heard of any of them before? Which do you think is the most impressive?

Shamu

Shamu is the stage name for a number of performing orcas at SeaWorld adventure parks. Wherever there is a SeaWorld, the Shamu show is always the most popular attraction. When you train an orca, you need lots of patience, lots of love – and lots of fish!

Bart the Bear

Bart the Bear was a nine-foot Alaskan Kodiak bear. When he was a cub, he was raised by humans and trained to act in films. Whenever actors worked with him, they were always impressed. He worked with stars such as Brad Pitt and Steven Seagal.

N'Kisi

N'Kisi's name is usually mentioned whenever experts talk about language use by animals. It is claimed that this African grey parrot can use over 950 words meaningfully. He takes part in scientific studies on interspecies communication.

B **Pair work** Discuss these questions and share your ideas with the class.

1. Do you think animals should be trained for entertainment? Is it ethical?

2. What other interesting talents or skills do animals have?

"I think it's OK to train animals as performers, provided that the animals have been rescued by people and not captured from the wild."

2 Helping hands

listening

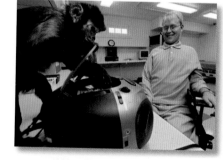

A Listen to these news reports on helper animals. What kinds of people does each animal help?

B Listen again. How does each animal help the people? Write *M* for monkey, *D* for dog, or *NG* for not given.

____ 1. fetching objects

____ 2. picking things up off the floor

____ 3. helping them to cross streets

____ 4. scratching an itchy nose

____ 5. giving them something to look forward to

____ 6. sparking memories of pets

____ 7. giving them something to take care of

____ 8. taking them places

____ 9. doing tricks to make them laugh

3 Whenever and wherever contrasted with when and where

grammar

Whenever and wherever mean "at any time" and "in any place." They are used to introduce adverbial clauses. Notice their position in the sentence.
Whenever experts talk about language use by animals, N'Kisi's name is usually mentioned.
N'Kisi's name is usually mentioned **whenever experts talk about language use by animals**.
Wherever there is a SeaWorld, the Shamu show is always the most popular attraction.
The Shamu show is always the most popular attraction **wherever there is a SeaWorld**.

Sometimes *when* and *where* can be used interchangeably with *whenever* and *wherever*.
Whenever / When actors worked with Bart the Bear, they were always impressed.
Wherever / Where there are performances by orcas, there are always a lot of spectators.

Whenever and *wherever* cannot be used if the sentence refers to a specific time or location.
Whenever actors worked with him, they were always impressed. (at any time)
When Brad Pitt worked with Bart in *Legends of the Fall*, he was very impressed. (specific time)
Wherever there are performances by orcas, there are always a lot of spectators. (any place)
The orcas were performing **where** there were a lot of spectators. (specific place)

Grammar Plus: See page 122.

A Look at the starting point on page 70 again. In which sentences can *whenever* and *wherever* be used interchangeably with *when* and *where*?

B Complete the sentences with *whenever* or *wherever*. If the time or place is specific, use *when* or *where*.

1. Large animals like tigers and bears need to be trained ＿＿＿＿＿＿＿ they are still very young.

2. Dogs are good traveling companions. They will go ＿＿＿＿＿＿＿ you take them.

3. ＿＿＿＿＿＿＿ someone has an unusual pet, serious problems can arise.

4. ＿＿＿＿＿＿＿ you see a dog wag its tail, you can assume it's happy. But ＿＿＿＿＿＿＿ a cat does the same thing, you should assume it's angry.

5. ＿＿＿＿＿＿＿ my sister lives, most people keep guard dogs to protect their property.

6. ＿＿＿＿＿＿＿ a messenger pigeon is taken and released, it can always find its way home.

C Match the clauses on the left with clauses on the right. Make logical sentences using *when, whenever, where,* or *wherever.*

1. We were very startled last night _c_
2. Parrots become very sad ＿＿
3. The sheep population grows quickly ＿＿
4. A guide dog always stops ＿＿
5. Police officers ride horses ＿＿
6. Our helper monkey wakes us up ＿＿

a. the traffic light is red.
b. they can't move quickly in cars.
c. a bat flew into the window.
d. there is plenty of grass to eat.
e. the sun comes up in the morning.
f. they are separated from people they love.

We were very startled last night when a bat flew into the window.

4 Physical features of animals

vocabulary

A Pair work Look at this list of animal body parts. Which type(s) of animal do they belong to? Write them in the correct column(s) in the chart.

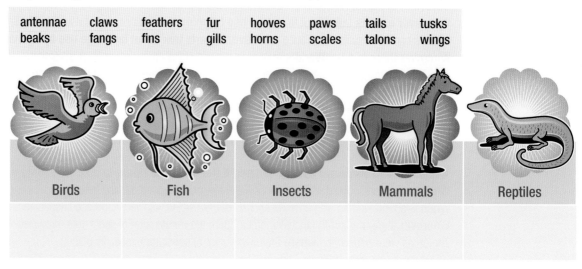

| antennae | claws | feathers | fur | hooves | paws | tails | tusks |
| beaks | fangs | fins | gills | horns | scales | talons | wings |

Birds	Fish	Insects	Mammals	Reptiles

B Pair work Think of two animals for each category. How are they the same? How are they different?

"Horses are an example of mammals with hooves. However, cats are mammals too, and they certainly don't have hooves. They have paws and claws."

5 Is it right to do that?

discussion

A Look at these ways humans use animals. How acceptable do you think they are? Add one idea of your own, and complete the chart.

ANIMAL ETHICS

	I'm against it.	I'm not sure.	I'm OK with it.
1. using ivory from elephant tusks in jewelry	☐	☐	☐
2. using rhinoceros horns for medicines	☐	☐	☐
3. using animals for medical research	☐	☐	☐
4. wearing animal fur and leather	☐	☐	☐
5. serving wild animal meat in restaurants	☐	☐	☐
6. using animals to test cosmetics	☐	☐	☐
7. training animals to perform in circuses	☐	☐	☐
8. _____	☐	☐	☐

B Group work Share your answers with the group, and explain your reasons. Who in your group seems to be the most "animal-friendly"?

"For most answers, I'm not sure. I don't want animals to be harmed, but if using animals for medical research can help us find a cure for cancer, then I'm inclined to support it."

6 Classification essay

writing

A classification essay organizes information into categories. The first paragraph includes a thesis statement and an overview of the categories. Each subsequent paragraph provides information about a single category. A conclusion gives an additional perspective on the overall topic.

A Read this draft of an essay. What categories of dogs does the writer mention?

Although most dogs offer their owners little more than companionship, assistance dogs are specially trained to assist people with disabilities or special needs. These dogs devote themselves to helping their owners live more independent lives. There are several types of assistance dogs, but the most common are guide dogs, hearing dogs, and service dogs.

Guide dogs help blind or visually impaired people get around their homes and communities. Most guide dogs are large breeds like German shepherds, which wear a harness with a U-shaped handle to allow the dog and its human partner to communicate. The owner gives directional commands, and the dog's role is to ensure the human's safety, even if it means disobeying an unsafe command.

Hearing dogs alert a person who is deaf or hearing-impaired to sounds like doorbells, baby cries, and smoke alarms. They're trained to make physical contact and lead their owner to the source of the sound. Hearing dogs are generally small to medium-sized mixed-breed dogs, and can be identified by their orange collar and vest.

Service dogs usually assist people who are confined to a wheelchair. The dogs are trained to pick up dropped objects, open and close doors, help in getting people into or out of a wheelchair, and find help when needed. Because many of these tasks require strength, most service dogs are large breeds such as golden or Labrador retrievers. These dogs usually wear a backpack or harness.

Guide dogs, hearing dogs, and service dogs have one thing in common, however. Before being matched with a human partner, each type of assistance dog undergoes a one- to two-year training program. Once the dog and owner are matched, they begin to form a bond of trust with each other and often become an inseparable team.

B Choose one of these topics or one of your own. Brainstorm ways to classify your topic into at least three categories, and make a list of ideas for each.

- pet owners
- types of cats
- types of pets
- types of friends

C Write a classification essay that includes an introduction, three or more paragraphs – each about a different category – and a conclusion.

D **Pair work** Read your partner's essay. Does it have a strong thesis? Are the categories distinct? Is each category described adequately? Do you have any suggestions for improvement?

Pet trends

starting point

A Read these blog comments about trends in the world of pets. Have you noticed these trends? What other pet trends have you noticed?

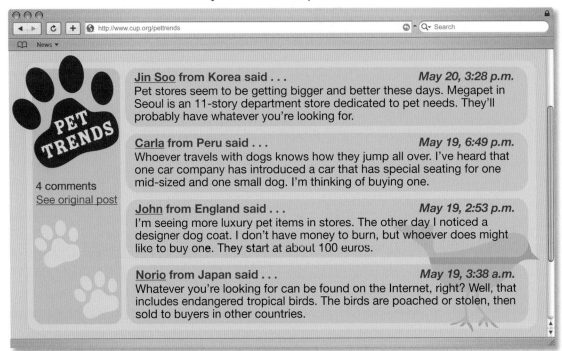

http://www.cup.org/pettrends

News ▼

PET TRENDS

4 comments
See original post

Jin Soo from Korea said . . .   *May 20, 3:28 p.m.*
Pet stores seem to be getting bigger and better these days. Megapet in Seoul is an 11-story department store dedicated to pet needs. They'll probably have whatever you're looking for.

Carla from Peru said . . .   *May 19, 6:49 p.m.*
Whoever travels with dogs knows how they jump all over. I've heard that one car company has introduced a car that has special seating for one mid-sized and one small dog. I'm thinking of buying one.

John from England said . . .   *May 19, 2:53 p.m.*
I'm seeing more luxury pet items in stores. The other day I noticed a designer dog coat. I don't have money to burn, but whoever does might like to buy one. They start at about 100 euros.

Norio from Japan said . . .   *May 19, 3:38 a.m.*
Whatever you're looking for can be found on the Internet, right? Well, that includes endangered tropical birds. The birds are poached or stolen, then sold to buyers in other countries.

B **Pair work** Discuss these questions with a partner.

1. What are some products and services that an 11-story pet store might provide?
2. How do you feel about putting clothing on pets?
3. What should be done about people who sell illegal exotic pets?

 Common ideas about pets

discussion

A Read these statements about pets. Check (✓) the statements you agree with.

Pet Pros and Cons

❏ **1.** Cats are cute when they're kittens, but they're unpleasant when they're older.

❏ **2.** Dogs and cats can't live in the same house. They fight whenever they are together.

❏ **3.** Taking a dog for a walk is a good way to relax whenever you feel tense.

❏ **4.** Dangerous exotic pets such as alligators should be outlawed, and whoever keeps them should be punished.

❏ **5.** Wherever there are pets, there is an increased risk of germs and disease.

B **Pair work** Discuss your answers with a partner. Are your ideas about pets the same or different?

3 Noun clauses with *whoever* and *whatever*

grammar

Whoever and *whatever* can begin noun clauses and function as either the subject or object of the clause.

Whoever = the person who / anyone who / everyone who
I don't have money to burn, but **whoever** does might like to buy one.
Whoever travels with dogs knows how they jump all over.

Whatever = anything that / everything that
They'll probably have **whatever** you're looking for.
Whatever you're looking for can be found on the Internet, right?

Grammar Plus: See page 123.

A Look at the starting point on page 74 again. In which sentences are *whoever* or *whatever* used as the subject of a clause? When are they the object of a clause?

B Complete the sentences with *whoever* or *whatever*. Then compare your answers with a partner.

1. Some cats are very curious. They have to investigate _____ their owners bring into the house.

2. _____ takes on the responsibility of owning a pet must provide food, water, shelter, and medical care for it.

3. _____ feeds wild animals is doing them a disservice, as giving them food can alter their feeding and migration patterns.

4. It's a good idea to own a guard dog that will bark at _____ approaches your house.

5. Guide dogs should be provided to _____ needs them.

6. People should do _____ is necessary to protect their pets.

7. Puppies seem to chew _____ they find around the house – shoes, clothing, even furniture.

8. Cats aren't always loyal to their owners – they become best friends with _____ pets them.

C **Group work** Complete the statements with your own ideas. Compare and discuss your ideas with your group.

1. Whoever has a strong desire to help stray animals . . .
   should consider volunteering some of their time at an animal shelter.

2. If you have a dog that doesn't listen and does whatever it wants, . . .

3. Cats make good pets for whoever . . .

4. It's a bad idea to feed a pet whatever it wants. Instead, . . .

5. Whoever wants a quiet pet . . .

4 Animal similes

vocabulary

A In English, we often describe people and their actions using similes that show animal characteristics. Complete the expressions with the most appropriate animal.

1. be as wise as __c__   a. a mouse
2. be as busy as ___   b. a dog
3. be as sick as ___   c. an owl
4. be as gentle as ___   d. a bee
5. be as strong as ___   e. a fox
6. be as quiet as ___   f. a mule
7. be as stubborn as ___   g. a lamb
8. be as sly as ___   h. an ox

B Look at these sentences. Use the expressions above to replace the phrase in boldface.

1. Beth seemed **so kind and soft-spoken** until she started yelling at the salesperson.

   Beth seemed as gentle as a lamb until she started yelling at the salesperson.

2. Maria couldn't make it to work today because she's **terribly ill**.

3. Juan is **so smart and sensible**. I always ask him for advice.

4. I can never tell whether my daughter Sarah is at home or not because she **hardly makes a sound**.

5. Pat easily convinces people to do whatever he wants. He's **quite clever and cunning**.

6. Whenever I need to lift something heavy, I always ask my son to help me because he **has extraordinary muscular strength**.

7. My sister never sits down – even on the weekend. She's **always occupied with some activity**.

8. It's a waste of time to discuss things with him. If he's convinced of something, he **refuses to change his** mind about it.

5 A suitable pet

listening

A Listen to a pet shop owner talk about suitable pets for different types of people. Write the types of people in the chart below.

B Listen again. What kind of pet is suitable for each type of person? Check (✓) the pets.

Type of person	Fish	Cat	Small dog	Parakeet	Large dog

A **Pair work** Do you think some pets could benefit from a psychologist? Discuss with a partner. Then read the article.

Kennel of the Mind

*H*ere in the United States, dogs get the **red-carpet treatment**. Sweaters for dogs. Hats for dogs. Doggy day care. So it only figures that dog psychologists are more in demand than ever.

Just another case of dog owners treating their pets like children? Actually, dog psychologists – or dog behaviorists, as some prefer – say dehumanizing confused, **over-babied** dogs is the bulk of their profession.

"With the projection of feelings that their dog is a human, owners are **doing an injustice** to the dog," says Rhonda Camfield, a practicing dog behaviorist based in Maroa, Illinois. "When the dog begins to believe that he or she is really a human, that's when the real problems surface."

By using **positive reinforcement** – a tactic that differentiates dog behaviorists from obedience schools – these professionals help disorderly canines settle into a more natural relationship between man and beast. And however silly that profession may seem, it's badly needed. "It's estimated that up to 90 percent of dogs in a shelter are there due to problem behavior, which could have been prevented," Camfield says. "Violent dogs make the news on a daily basis, and we put thousands of dogs to sleep every day across the U.S."

Thus, dog psychologists not only protect an owner from a volatile dog, they can save such a dog from being **euthanized**. Only in the big cities, right? Well, no, actually. High-profile dog behaviorists **litter the map**, from small suburbs to rural **backwaters**. "People are willing to travel to save the dog they love," Camfield says. "I'm in a small town, central Illinois. Dogs have come to me from several states."

And it's easy to get started. "In the U.S., you do not need to be certified to be a dog trainer," says Dave Lorch, a canine behavior trainer in New Orleans for two years. Lorch recommends aspiring behaviorists "look for someone who currently trains dogs to **apprentice** with. Research a number of different methods – no one method is better than another." 🐾

Source: "Kennel of the mind," by Drew Hinshaw, *Metro New York*

B **Pair work** Write the expressions and words in boldface next to their definitions.

1. constructive feedback _____
2. pampered, coddled _____
3. spoiled; treated like royalty _____
4. being unfair; mistreating _____
5. train under someone _____
6. put to death _____
7. a remote place _____
8. be everywhere _____

C **Group work** Discuss these questions. Then share your answers with the class.

1. Do you think animals can have humanlike qualities or emotions?
2. Why are owners doing their dogs an injustice by giving them human qualities? What kinds of problems do you think this can cause?
3. Would you bring your pet to a psychologist? Why or why not?

How well can you do these things? Rate your ability from 1 to 5 (1 = low, 5 = high).

Discuss trends using relative pronouns and adjectives with negative prefixes (Ex. 1)	_____
Describe ways of marketing new products using the subjunctive (Ex. 2)	_____
Discuss animals and give opinions on if they would be suitable as pets (Ex. 3)	_____
Listen to a radio interview using *whoever* and direct and indirect objects (Ex. 4)	_____

Now do the corresponding exercises below. Were your ratings correct?

Trends and attitudes

discussion

A **Pair work** Read what these people have to say about recent trends. Who do you agree with the most, and who do you agree with the least? Discuss your ideas with a partner, and give reasons for them.

CARLOS

"I think it's great that so many companies allow employees to telecommute. It's illogical, even irresponsible, for companies to require employees who don't live nearby to come in to work every day."

LIN

"Something that worries me is the way people risk their health by experimenting with alternative medicines and therapies that haven't been properly tested. No one really knows how safe they are."

STEPHANIE

"I'm hoping attitudes toward consumption – like constantly buying new clothes – are changing. Celebrities like actors, musicians, and athletes, whom young people look up to, need to set the right example and start facilitating change."

"I disagree with Lin. I don't think alternative medicines are dangerous. Many of them are traditional medicines that have been used for years."

B **Group work** Discuss how you feel about these life choices. Then share your answers with the class.

- adult children returning home to live with their parents
- people choosing to adopt children rather than having children of their own
- people using the Internet for social networking
- senior citizens going back to school to earn degrees
- people choosing to spend more of their free time doing volunteer work

2 New products and marketing plans

discussion

A Group work Think of a new product or service you think would be successful. What is it? Who is it for? How does it work? What's the best way to advertise and promote it?

"Well, I'm thinking about a concierge service for people who are new in town. The concierge could provide the same services as a concierge in a hotel."

"I suggest we offer information and advice to help them cope with all the changes that living in a new community brings."

"Good idea. I recommend we advertise on the town's website . . ."

B Present your product or service and advertising plans to the class. Which group has the best ideas?

3 Suitable pets?

speaking

A Would you consider keeping any of these animals as pets? Why or why not?

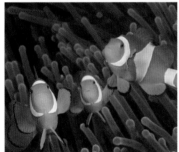
tropical fish

boa constrictor

chimpanzee

B Pair work Compare your ideas with a partner. Explain your reasons.

"I really love tropical fish. Whenever I get the chance, I go snorkeling. I wouldn't keep them as pets, though. I would rather see them in the ocean than in an aquarium."

4 Bird talk

listening

A 🔘 Listen to an interview with a parrot expert. She mentions three things that are important for a person to have before getting an African grey parrot. Check (✓) the three basic requirements she mentions.

☐ a. time   ☐ c. space   ☐ e. children

☐ b. a DVD   ☐ d. interest in parrots   ☐ f. asthma

B 🔘 Listen again. Are these statements true or false? Check (✓) the correct answer.

	True	False
1. It is illegal to import wild African grey parrots.	☐	☐
2. Parrots cause asthma.	☐	☐
3. Parrots are intelligent and unpredictable.	☐	☐
4. Parrots need some time outside of their cage each day.	☐	☐
5. Research has been done on African grey parrots talking.	☐	☐
6. Parrots can eat all fruits and vegetables.	☐	☐

LESSON A · Communication skills

1 Effective communicators

starting point

A Read about these effective communicators. What else do you know about them?

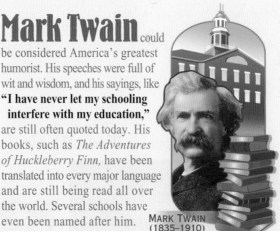

Mark Twain could be considered America's greatest humorist. His speeches were full of wit and wisdom, and his sayings, like **"I have never let my schooling interfere with my education,"** are still often quoted today. His books, such as *The Adventures of Huckleberry Finn,* have been translated into every major language and are still being read all over the world. Several schools have even been named after him.

MARK TWAIN (1835–1910)

No one should have been surprised when **Nelson Mandela** was awarded the Nobel Peace Prize in 1993. Even while in prison for 27 years, his fight to end apartheid in South Africa was being kept alive by activists around the world. Mandela is always going to be remembered for his great speeches and eloquent quotations, such as, **"Education is the most powerful weapon which you can use to change the world."**

NELSON MANDELA (1918–)

B **Pair work** Who are some other effective communicators? Why are they effective?

2 Fear of public speaking

discussion

A Studies have shown that public speaking is most people's biggest fear. Do you share this fear? Complete the survey. Add a statement of your own.

Are you **afraid** to talk?

	Always true	Sometimes true	Never true
1. I can't sleep the night before a presentation.	☐	☐	☐
2. I rarely participate in discussions at work or in class.	☐	☐	☐
3. I avoid situations in which I might have to give an impromptu speech.	☐	☐	☐
4. When talking to others, I find it hard to look people in the eye.	☐	☐	☐
5. I can speak only from a prepared speech.	☐	☐	☐
6. I am intimidated by job interviews.	☐	☐	☐
7. I'd rather go to the dentist, pay taxes, or clean closets than give a presentation.	☐	☐	☐
8. _____	☐	☐	☐

Source: Schaum's Quick Guide to Great Presentation Skills

B **Pair work** Compare your answers. What do you have in common? How are you different?

3 Overview of passives

grammar

Passive sentences focus on the receiver of the action by making it the subject of the sentence. The agent that performs the action can be omitted or follow *by* after the verb.

Passive = subject + form of *be* + past participle (+ *by* + agent)

Simple present: Mark Twain's sayings **are** still often **quoted** today (by scholars).

Present continuous: Twain's books **are** still **being read** all over the world.

Present perfect: Twain's books **have been translated** into every major language.

Simple past: Nelson Mandela **was awarded** the Nobel Peace Prize in 1993.

Past continuous: Mandela's fight **was being kept** alive (by activists) around the world.

Future with *going to*: Mandela **is** always **going to be remembered** for his great speeches.

Modals: Mark Twain **could be considered** America's greatest humorist.

Past modals: No one **should have been surprised**.

Grammar Plus: See page 124.

A Look at the starting point on page 80 again. Can you find another example of the passive? What verb form is it in?

B Change these active sentences to the passive. Keep or omit the agent as appropriate.

1. The Internet has changed the way the world communicates.

   The way the world communicates has been changed by the Internet.

2. People should deliver wedding speeches confidently and cheerfully.

3. Someone should have told the students to speak louder during their speeches.

4. Many counselors are advising married couples to communicate more openly.

5. Long ago, people used smoke signals to send simple messages in China.

6. After the ceremony, the president is announcing the scholarship recipients.

7. Translators are going to translate the president's speech into 35 languages.

8. The principal was making an announcement when the microphone went dead.

C Complete these sentences with information about language that is true for you. Then add another sentence of your own using a passive verb form.

1. I've been told by many people that . . .

   my English sounds quite formal.

2. My classmates and I are encouraged to . . .

3. I hope that someday I will be offered . . .

4. Not long ago, I was told that . . .

5. Languages should be taught . . .

6. I've been advised . . .

7. Students should / shouldn't be forced to . . .

8. _____

Total Insurance

4 Discourse markers

vocabulary

A Discourse markers are expressions that make communication flow more smoothly. Match each expression below with a function it serves.

a. to open a presentation   c. to add information   e. to introduce contrasts

b. to sequence information   d. to introduce similarities   f. to close a presentation

___ 1. in conclusion   E 5. nevertheless   *Sin embargo*   D 9. likewise

___ 2. next   C 6. in addition   E 10. yet

___ 3. similarly   F 7. to sum up   B 11. first / second / third

A 4. to begin   B 8. first of all   C 12. furthermore

B **Pair work** Complete each sentence with an expression from Exercise A. Sometimes more than one answer is possible.

(1) _To begin of_, let me thank everyone for your interest and attention as I speak on the topic of petroleum dependency – our dependency on oil for our energy needs. *need to much.*

    There are several reasons why we should be concerned about our dependency on petroleum. (2) _first of all_, petroleum-based fuels contribute to both air pollution and global warming, two very serious problems today. (3) _In addition_, there is a limited supply of oil in the world; therefore, we must be prepared to replace petroleum with other sources of energy. There are many ways in which to do this on a large scale. First, we must produce fuel-efficient cars; (4) _next_, we must encourage the use of public transportation. Finally, tax breaks could be offered to businesses that conserve fuel. *combustible* (5) _Similarly_, homeowners could also be offered tax incentives for fuel conservation. It's true that cutting down on consumption is beneficial to the environment; (6) _nevertheless_, we should keep in mind that cutting down too quickly could have a negative effect on the economy.

    (7) _To Sum up_, this problem has no simple answers, but if the government, corporations, and private citizens all work together, I feel we can solve the problem.

5 Getting your message across

listening

A Listen to advice about speaking in public. Check (✓) the items the speaker mentions in the chart below.

B Listen again. Complete the chart with the advice you hear.

	Advice			Advice
☐ the audience			☐ posture	
☐ the outline			☐ eye contact	
☐ pronunciation			☐ voice	
☐ practicing			☐ questions	
☐ humor			☐ speed	

6 Persuasive writing

writing

> In persuasive writing, you take a position on an issue and try to convince the reader that your position is correct. To do so, you should provide examples and reasons that support your case, as well as present the opposing point of view and argue against it.

A Read the following composition. What is the writer's position? What are the reasons the writer gives to support the position? Do you think the writer's case is convincing?

Every Student Should Be Required to Study a Foreign Language

 Recently, a student organization at our university proposed that we do away with our foreign language requirement, which mandates that all students complete two years of foreign language study. The main reason for this proposal seems to be to eliminate unnecessary courses; however, the proponents of this change are overlooking the great benefits foreign language study provides to students of any major.

Students who oppose the language requirement argue that university study should be more career focused. They feel that the language requirement steals time that could be spent on courses directly related to a student's major. This is a shortsighted position. Statistics show that bilingual candidates have an increased chance of getting jobs . . .

Another point often made by the proponents of the change is that a large number of students who study a language for two years rarely use it again in their lives. While this may be true in some cases, study of a foreign language has been shown to increase proficiency in one's native language. Similarly, the understanding of oneself and one's own culture is increased through contact with another language and its culture . . .

In conclusion, it is crucial that we keep the foreign language requirement. To eliminate it would be doing a great disservice to our university and its students. Foreign language learning benefits us in concrete and subtle ways as it broadens our minds and expands our opportunities.

–James Baker

B **Pair work** With a partner, take a position on one of these issues related to language, or use your own idea. Then brainstorm reasons supporting this position.

- Schools should teach a second language starting in kindergarten.
- Every student should be required to study abroad.
- Institutions should be created to preserve and conserve languages.

C Write a multiparagraph composition supporting your position with the reasons you have brainstormed. Make sure you argue against the opposing position.

D **Pair work** Take turns reading your compositions. Suggest ways your partner's writing could be made more persuasive.

What's correct language?

A Read these statements about language, and check (✓) the statements you agree with.

Proper English

☐ 1. Most people don't need to write well. Speaking is more important.

☐ 2. The majority of teenagers use too much slang.

☐ 3. Three-quarters of e-mail messages contain grammar errors.

☐ 4. No one expects e-mail to be correct.

☐ 5. There are plenty of people with accents who speak English well.

☐ 6. None of us has the right to correct other people's grammar.

☐ 7. All varieties of English are equally valid. Every variety is correct.

☐ 8. A lot of advanced grammar is complicated even for native speakers.

☐ 9. Only a minority of my friends cares about speaking correctly.

starting point

Please use Spell check!

B **Pair work** Discuss your opinions with a partner.

"I disagree with the first sentence. A lot of people need to write well for their jobs."

Text speak

discussion

A **Pair work** Read about the phenomenon of "text speak." Then try to figure out what the six examples of text speak mean, and write the meaning. (For the answers, turn to page 152.)

> **"Text speak"** refers to shortened forms of words used primarily in text-messaging. When texting began, telephone companies would charge by the word, so fewer words and letters meant cheaper messages. These days, many young people find text speak convenient and cool, and it is creeping into e-mails and even classroom work. Examples of text speak include:
>
> B4 __before__   CUL8R _____   GR8 _____
>
> RUOK _____   XLNT _____   2NITE _____

B **Group work** Read these opinions about text speak. Which one do you most agree with? Discuss your opinions about text speak with the group.

I try not to use text speak – except in text messaging, of course – because it's annoying. I think people who use it in schoolwork and in e-mails look idiotic and immature. –Raphael [Reply]	People are free to use text speak if they think it's more convenient – after all, it's a free country. But, I do hope it remains an alternative style, and that grammar is maintained. –Su Jin [Reply]
Txt spk is gr8! It's much easier and quicker, and u can use it for e-mail, taking notes in class, writing letters, and even in some homework assignments. –Wendy [Reply]	I really feel old when my younger sister writes to me using text speak, and I'm only 24! Nevertheless, I know that language always evolves. Just think of the difference between our English and Shakespeare's! –Rob [Reply]

3 Subject-verb agreement with quantifiers

grammar

All (of), a lot of, lots of, plenty of, some (of), most (of), and fractions take a singular verb if the noun they modify is uncountable or singular. They take a plural verb if the noun they modify is plural.
Most people don't need to write well.
Three-quarters of e-mail **messages contain** grammar errors.
A lot of advanced grammar **is** complicated.

Each of, every one of, none of, and collective nouns, such as *majority (of)* and *minority (of),* typically take a singular verb, but often take a plural verb after a plural noun in informal speech.
The **majority of** teenagers **use / uses** too much slang.
A **minority of** my friends **care / cares** about speaking correctly.
None of us has / have the right to correct other people's grammar.

Everyone, someone, anyone, no one, each + noun, and *every* + noun are followed by a singular verb.
Every variety **is** correct.
No one expects e-mail to be correct.

Grammar Plus: See page 125.

A Look at the starting point on page 84 again. Can you find other quantifiers? Are they followed by a singular or plural verb?

B Complete these sentences with the correct form of the verb in parentheses.

1. A lot of people ____agree____ that spelling and grammar shouldn't change. (agree)

2. All of the students in my class _____ English club meetings. (attend)

3. Most of the faculty at school _____ at least three languages. (speak)

4. A quarter of my classmates _____ going to study abroad next semester. (be)

5. The majority of people _____ text speak in their e-mails. (use)

6. None of the information in the e-mail _____ correct. (be)

7. Every letter I receive usually _____ one or two spelling mistakes. (contain)

8. A lot of the language that people use every day _____ inappropriate in writing. (be)

C **Group work** Complete these sentences with information about how people use language in different situations. Then discuss your answers.

1. A lot of the slang people use these days . . .
2. The majority of people my age . . .
3. A lot of the language older people use . . .
4. None of my friends . . .
5. Most of the news anchors you see on TV . . .
6. Every one of my teachers . . .

"A lot of the slang people use these days comes from popular music."

"That's true. In hip-hop slang, 'crib' means home, and 'bling' means flashy jewelry."

4 Idiomatic expressions

vocabulary

A The expressions on the left can be used to comment on people and the way they speak. Match them with their definitions on the right.

1. have a sharp tongue _e_
2. have a way with words _h_
3. hem and haw _A_
4. stick to the point _D_
5. talk behind someone's back _C_
6. talk someone into something _f_
7. talk someone's ear off _G_
8. love to hear oneself talk _B_

a. talk indecisively; avoid saying something directly
b. enjoy talking even if nobody is listening
c. talk about people without their knowing
d. continue talking about a main idea
e. talk in a bitter, critical way
f. convince a person to do something
g. talk until the other person is tired of listening
h. have a talent for speaking

B **Pair work** Use expressions from above to comment on these people and the way they are speaking.

1. Klaus

"I wouldn't say I dislike him, or at least I don't think so. I guess it's hard to say."

2. Risa

"Why don't you want to go? Come on! It'll be fun, and it's cheap. I'll even drive!"

3. Sandra

"Just be quiet! You don't know what you're talking about, so stop wasting my time!"

4. Philip

"Diane got an F on her test. She tried to put it away quickly, but I saw it anyway!"

5 Assert yourself!

listening & speaking

A Listen to three rather one-sided conversations. Write the number of the conversation beside each description.

____ a. One person is talking the other person's ear off.

____ b. One person is trying to talk the other person into doing something.

____ c. One person isn't sticking to the point.

B Listen again. Which expressions do you hear used in the conversations? Write the number of the conversation beside each expression.

____ a. Could I say something?
____ b. Thanks for asking, but . . .
____ c. I just wanted to say . . .

____ d. That's nice, but we really need to . . .
____ e. That's really nice of you, but . . .
____ f. Getting back to what we were talking about . . .

C **Pair work** Prepare a dialogue similar to those from the listening. Use the expressions above. Then perform the scene for the class.

6. English varieties

A **Pair work** Read the quote in the first line of the article. What do you think it means? Then read the article to compare your ideas to the author's.

Slang Abroad

George Bernard Shaw said, "England and America are two countries separated by a common language." I never really understood the meaning of this quote until a friend and I stopped in a London convenience store. We had some trash to throw away, so I, in as polite a manner as I could muster, asked the clerk for a trash can. Then I asked him again, thinking he didn't hear me. And then I asked again, only this time while speaking the international language (loudly and slowly while pointing to the object I wanted to throw away). After this horribly rude display, he politely asked me what a trash can was. So I told him it was a place for my garbage. I guess this weak explanation worked. The clerk then produced a small trash can from behind the counter and in the most you-must-not-be-from-around-here tone he could muster said, "rubbish bin."

Different names for objects, however, is not the main problem. Anyone can learn a language. But to really be a speaker of the language, you need to understand its idioms and its slang. There is a distinct difference between someone who learned a language in a classroom and someone who is a native speaker. Using slang proves that the speaker has been in a country long enough to learn it, and that offers a benefit greater than just being able to converse on a casual level. It allows the two speakers to get much closer much more quickly.

Eventually, after living somewhere for a while you pick up a few things, and this new language education gives a credibility that just pronouncing a city address cannot. It shows a belonging and membership in the club of permanent residents and that one is not just a mere extended tourist. I know it sounds superficial, that by being able to understand words that may or may not be in a dictionary, we can fool people into thinking we belong, but it isn't. What knowing and using slang shows is a basic understanding of a culture. It offers both members of the conversation a common ground.

And that's the point. Britain and America are two countries separated by a common language, but then again so are Mexico and Spain, Brazil and Portugal, and France and Haiti. While these countries' languages may all seem the same on paper, they're not. Really learning the languages can only be done on the ground. And once that learning is done, something far greater is achieved than just not sounding like a fool.

Source: "Slang abroad," by Ben Falk, *The Daily Colonial.*

B Which of these statements would the author probably agree with? Compare and discuss your answers.

1. Knowing one variety of a language doesn't mean you can speak it everywhere.
2. Studying books about slang is an effective way to learn how it's used.
3. Idiomatic use of language is a superficial part of a country's culture.
4. Really learning a language means learning how local people actually use it.

C **Group work** Discuss these questions. Then share your answers with the class.

1. Do you agree with the author's idea that one can only really learn a language by living in a country where it's spoken? Why or why not?
2. Have you ever had any experiences like the one in the first paragraph? What happened? Do you think such misunderstandings are common?

11 Exceptional people

LESSON A · High achievers

1 They had an impact!

starting point

A Read about the exceptional people below. Have you heard of any of these people? What sort of impact have they had on other people?

Mahatma Gandhi

(1869–1948) Gandhi was a great political and spiritual leader in India. Although he was educated in England, Gandhi is best remembered for his struggle for Indian independence, which had far-reaching effects. His epoch-making victories through peaceful means later inspired other great leaders, like Martin Luther King, Jr., and Aung San Suu Kyi.

Natalia Vodianova

(1982–) Born in Russia, this blue-eyed, brown-haired beauty was working in a fruit stand by age 11. At 15, she joined a modeling academy and soon after moved to Paris, where she was well received and quickly became a popular fashion model. A kind-hearted superstar, she created the Naked Heart Foundation to build playgrounds for underprivileged children in Russia.

Pelé

(1940–) A Brazilian soccer player, Pelé (Edison Arantes do Nascimento) is a well-known athlete all over the world. He won his first World Cup with Brazil when he was only 17 years old. His universally praised playing style and athleticism have never been matched. Considered a pioneer of modern soccer, he is also known for his painstaking dedication to improving social conditions for the poor.

B **Group work** Think of people who have had an impact on the world. Discuss their achievements, then choose the person who has had the biggest impact.

2 Exceptional values

discussion

A Think about the people you talked about in the starting point above. What values do you think were most important to each of them?

"I think Gandhi valued patience. He had patience with people and patience to achieve his goal through nonviolent measures."

B Look at this list of life values. Check (✓) the three that are the most important in your life. If your top values aren't here, add them to the list.

- ☐ achievement
- ☐ being a "team player"
- ☐ concern for others
- ☐ creativity
- ☐ health
- ☐ independence
- ☐ money
- ☐ responsibility
- ☐ spirituality
- ☐ the environment
- ☐ _____
- ☐ _____

C **Group work** Discuss your choices with the members of your group. Then make a list of the three life values that are the most important to your group as a whole.

3 Compound adjectives

grammar

Compound adjectives are modifying phrases made up of two or more words. They can be joined by a hyphen, appear as a single word, or appear as two separate words. Always check your dictionary before using compound adjectives in writing.

Three common patterns for compound adjectives in English are:

a. adjective + noun + -ed *(absent-minded, high-spirited, long-winded, soft-hearted)*
When preceding a noun, these compounds are usually written with a hyphen unless they are one word.

b. adverb + past participle *(much-loved, well-dressed, highly acclaimed, widely respected)*
Compounds with adverbs ending in -ly are never hyphenated. Other adverbs are usually hyphenated before but not after the noun.

c. adjective, adverb, or noun + present participle *(easygoing, forward-looking, thought-provoking)*
When preceding a noun, these compounds are usually written with a hyphen unless they are one word.

Grammar Plus: See page 126.

A Look at the starting point on page 88 again. Can you find more compound adjectives? Which patterns from the grammar box do they follow?

B Rewrite these sentences using the compound adjectives from the starting point to replace the words in boldface. Sometimes more than one answer is possible.

1. Tiger Woods is a golfer **everybody knows**.

   Tiger Woods is a well-known golfer.

2. The play, which was **praised by every critic in the city**, is sold out.

3. Many charities are set up to help children **who are poor**.

4. The **very generous** celebrity gave money to the homeless.

5. The work of Gandhi had effects **that reached around the world**.

6. The child **with brown eyes** was adopted by a celebrity.

4 Compound adjectives related to the body

vocabulary

A Pair work Combine the words from both boxes to create compound adjectives. How many combinations can you think of?

absent *(ausente)*	cool	hard	narrow	soft	blooded	hearted
cold	empty *(vacio)*	hot	open	warm	headed	minded

B Match the compound adjectives you created to their synonyms below. Sometimes more than one answer is possible.

1. silly and brainless _empty-headed_ *(tonto)*
2. quick to anger _hot blooded_ -hot headed *(colera)*
3. uncaring or unkind _cold hearted_ *(indiferente cruel)*
4. sweet and loving _soft hearted_ -warm hearted open hearted
5. stubborn and unyielding _cool headed_ *(terco)* inflexible hard headed.
6. tolerant and unbiased _open minded_ *(imparcial bais-d)*
7. intolerant and disapproving _narrow minded_
8. forgetful _absent minded_
9. calm and unexcitable _Cool headed._
10. friendly and kind _warm hearted_

5. Do you want to be a high achiever?

listening

A 🔘 Listen to a motivational speaker talk about the qualities of high achievers. Check (✓) the four qualities he talks about in the chart below.

B 🔘 Listen again. What does the speaker suggest people do in order to build the four qualities of high achievers? Write the suggestions in the chart.

	Suggestion		Suggestion
☐ lifelong learning		☐ positive attitude	
☐ high self-esteem		☐ risk-taking	
☐ responsibility		☐ creativity	

6. Memorable quotations

discussion

A **Pair work** Read these quotations from exceptional people. Can you restate these quotations in your own words?

Eleanor Roosevelt
(1884–1963)
American humanitarian

"I believe that anyone can conquer fear by doing the things he fears to do."

Lao Tzu
(c. 600 BC–c. 470 BC)
Chinese sage

"A journey of a thousand miles begins with a single step."

Thomas Edison
American inventor

"Genius is one percent inspiration and ninety-nine percent perspiration."

Gertrude Stein
(1874–1946)
American author

"We are always the same age inside."

Mahatma Gandhi
(1869–1948)
Indian leader

"Learn as if you were going to live forever."

> **Useful expressions**
>
> **Describing what something means**
> What this means to me is that . . .
> My understanding of this is that . . .
> I interpret this to mean . . .

B **Group work** Which of the quotations above might be useful for the following kinds of people? Do you know any other sayings or quotations that might be helpful?

1. someone who wants to write a book and become an author
2. someone who wants to learn another language, but can't speak one word yet
3. someone who wants to study abroad but is afraid to live in a foreign country
4. someone who thinks he or she is too old to travel abroad
5. someone who is hesitant to register for a class because of a lack of time

7 Biographical profile

> A biographical profile usually begins with an introduction that includes a thesis statement about what makes the person interesting or special. The subsequent paragraphs are then usually arranged in chronological order.

A The paragraphs in this biographical profile about J. K. Rowling have been scrambled. Read the composition and put the paragraphs in order.

☐   Rowling received a grant allowing her to finish the book in 1995, but it was rejected by 15 publishers before a small company called Bloomsbury published it in 1997. In 1998, the book was published in the United States as *Harry Potter and the Sorcerer's Stone*. It wasn't long before the book was winning awards and rising to the top of the bestsellers lists. Rowling went on to write and publish the second book in the series in 1999, and then several more in the seven-book series between then and 2007. Today she's the bestselling author of all time.

☐   Born in Gloucestershire, England, in 1965, Rowling was a good student whose favorite subjects were English and foreign languages, and after graduating from high school she studied French at Exeter University. Following her graduation from Exeter, Rowling worked as a bilingual secretary. On a train trip during this time, Rowling got the idea for a book about a boy named Harry Potter, an orphan who learns he is a wizard and enters a school of wizardry and witchcraft. Rowling began writing the book during lunch breaks and meetings, before finally quitting her job at age 26 and moving to Portugal to work as an English teacher.

☐   If you don't know who J. K. Rowling is, you must be from another planet. Her Harry Potter books have been translated into 28 languages and are sold in 115 countries. They have been turned into popular movies. Although Rowling has earned over one billion dollars for her work and has been called a genius by many, life wasn't always easy for her.

☐   In Portugal, Rowling's schedule allowed her to write during the mornings, and she continued working on the book. While there she married a Portuguese journalist, but after the birth of their daughter, Rowling returned to England with a suitcase full of Harry Potter notes. She continued to write, and went to a café with her daughter every day to work on her Harry Potter book.

B Choose a famous person you know a lot about. Make notes and list events from this person's life in chronological order. Then use your notes to write a biographical profile.

C **Pair work** Exchange profiles with a partner, and answer these questions.

1. Does your partner's profile begin with an introduction and include a thesis statement?
2. Is the information in the profile arranged in chronological order?
3. Can you suggest any improvements to make the profile more interesting or effective?
4. What else would you like to know about the person your partner wrote about?

LESSON B · People we admire

1 Role models

A Read these posts about role models on an Internet discussion board. What life values are reflected in each of the posts?

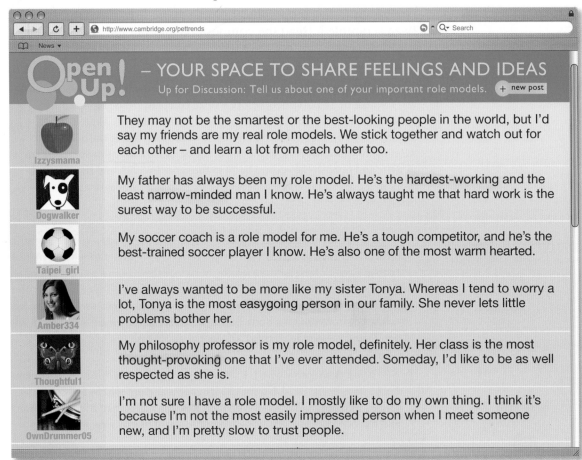

— YOUR SPACE TO SHARE FEELINGS AND IDEAS

Up for Discussion: Tell us about one of your important role models. + new post

Izzysmama
They may not be the smartest or the best-looking people in the world, but I'd say my friends are my real role models. We stick together and watch out for each other – and learn a lot from each other too.

Dogwalker
My father has always been my role model. He's the hardest-working and the least narrow-minded man I know. He's always taught me that hard work is the surest way to be successful.

Taipei_girl
My soccer coach is a role model for me. He's a tough competitor, and he's the best-trained soccer player I know. He's also one of the most warm hearted.

Amber334
I've always wanted to be more like my sister Tonya. Whereas I tend to worry a lot, Tonya is the most easygoing person in our family. She never lets little problems bother her.

Thoughtful1
My philosophy professor is my role model, definitely. Her class is the most thought-provoking one that I've ever attended. Someday, I'd like to be as well respected as she is.

OwnDrummer05
I'm not sure I have a role model. I mostly like to do my own thing. I think it's because I'm not the most easily impressed person when I meet someone new, and I'm pretty slow to trust people.

B **Pair work** Create a post for the discussion board about one of your important role models. Share it with the class.

"My grandfather is a very important role model in my life. He started his own business when he was 18 years old . . ."

2 People who make a difference

A Listen to Luisa talk about her grandmother and Chu-lan talk about his parents. How do Luisa and Chu-lan feel about the people they are describing?

B Listen again. In what ways did these people influence Luisa and Chu-lan? Write two ways for each.

How did Luisa's grandmother influence her?	How did Chu-lan's parents influence him?
1.	1.
2.	2.

3 Superlative compound adjectives

grammar

Superlative compound adjectives generally follow the same hyphenation rules as compound adjectives.

The superlative form of compound adjectives is most often formed by adding *the most* and *the least*. There is never a hyphen after *most* or *least*.
I'm not **the most easily impressed** person.
Tonya is **the most easygoing** person in our family.
He's the **least narrow-minded** man I know.

The superlative form of a compound adjective can also be formed by adding *the* and *-est* to an adjective or adverb having one or sometimes two syllables.
He is **the hardest-working** man.
They may not be the smartest or **the best-looking people** in the world.

Compound adjectives in their superlative form can also occur after the verb *be* without a noun.
Of all the men I know, he's the **hardest working**.   *Grammar Plus: See page 127.*

A Look at the starting point on page 92 again. How many superlative compound adjectives can you find?

B Rewrite these phrases using the superlative form of the compound adjective.

1. an awe-inspiring place
2. a widely read book
3. a good-looking man
4. a thirst-quenching beverage
5. a highly developed mind
6. a warm-hearted friend
7. a far-sighted plan
8. a thought-provoking novel
9. a well-defined project
10. a bad-intentioned person

C Complete these sentences with the superlative compound adjectives you wrote above and your own ideas. Share your answers with a partner.

1 . . . natural place I've ever been to is . . .
   The most awe-inspiring natural place I've ever been to is the Grand Canyon.
2. . . . newspaper in the country is probably . . .
3. In my opinion, . . . actor / actress in the world is . . .
4. On a hot day, . . . drink is . . .
5. . . . movie I've ever seen is . . .
6. . . . person I know is . . .
7. . . . leader my country has ever had is / was . . .

4 Phrasal verbs

vocabulary

A Read the sentences below. Then match the phrasal verbs in boldface with their definitions.

a. take care of   e. confront *face to face*
Protect b. defend or support   f. experience *patience*
Same c. go see if someone is all right   g. resemble (a parent) in looks or character
     Confront d. rely on   h. perform in a way equal to expectations

__D__ 1. It's only natural for children to **look to** their parents for advice.

__F__ 2. Life isn't all good times; we need to **go through** difficulties too.

__C__ 3. Before parents go to bed, they should **check on** their kids and see if they're OK.

__E__ 4. Parents need to teach their children to **face up to** their problems and solve them.

__A__ 5. I expect my children to **look after** me when I reach old age.

__B__ 6. Whenever I argue with my sister, it seems like my mother and father **side with** her.

__H__ 7. The children of accomplished parents often find it difficult to **live up to** the high expectations people have for them.

__G__ 8. When it comes to finances, I **take after** my dad; he could never save money either.

B **Pair work** Discuss the sentences in Exercise A with a partner. Comment on the statements, and talk about how they apply to your life situation.

"I find that the older I get, the more I look to my parents for advice."

5 Everyday heroism

discussion

A **Pair work** Read what Farah says about heroic behavior. What is her definition of a hero? Do you agree with the definition? Do you have other examples?

To me, heroes often aren't the most widely recognized people, and on the surface their actions don't necessarily seem to be the most awe inspiring. A hero could be a parent who, after an exhausting day, helps a child with a difficult homework assignment. It could be a person on the street who picks up and returns something you didn't realize you'd dropped, someone who stops by to check on you when you're ill, someone who sides with you when you've been wronged, someone who takes time out of a busy schedule to help you with a problem. A hero is not just a person who has the courage to take a risk; he or she is also a person who has the courage to always be kind to people no matter what they're going through.

Farah, 26

B **Group work** Discuss these situations. What would you do to make a difference?

a Your next-door neighbor fell and broke her leg. She lives by herself.

b The condition of your neighborhood park has deteriorated, and fewer and fewer people are using it.

c Children in a nearby low-income neighborhood seem to have few opportunities for academic success.

d A friend of yours has lost his or her job and can't seem to find another one.

"I would check on her from time to time and help her with some of her daily chores."

6. A champion for women in Africa

reading

A **Pair work** Do you know any nongovernment organizations (NGOs)? Discuss some of the ways they are making a change. Then read the article.

ANN COTTON, SOCIAL ENTREPRENEUR

The following is an interview from a British newspaper with Ann Cotton, founder and chief executive of the Campaign for Female Education (Camfed), an NGO which currently helps over 250,000 women in Zimbabwe, Zambia, Ghana, and Tanzania.

How do you define a social entrepreneur? Someone who witnesses the pain and struggle in the lives of others and is compelled to act and to work with them.

What skills are needed to be a social entrepreneur? You need to be absolutely dogged. You need to listen to the people experiencing the problems, and their ideas need to crowd out the words of the "can't be done-ers."

How did your work as a former teacher and head of children's assessment help in setting up Camfed? There will always be children who don't fit the institution and whose sense of exclusion is reinforced day by day. Their experience shaped my approach to children and young people in Africa.

How did you learn how to run a successful charity? I learned by doing, and from others who were encouraging and generous in their help. I belonged to a community of activists that was inspirational.

How did you manage the growth of Camfed from supporting 32 girls, with £2,000 raised from selling your homemade cakes, to a £3,000,000 NGO? Lucy Lake, now deputy executive director, and I built the whole model from the grass roots up. Donors could see it was working and began to get behind us in increasing numbers. We attract and retain outstanding individuals. In Africa, the early beneficiaries head the programs – young women who share a background of rural poverty, transformation through education, and the courage to bring about change.

What has been the key to the success of Camfed? Never take your eye off the ball. Always remember that you and everyone on the team is the servant of the cause – in our case, girls' education and young women's leadership in Africa.

What advice would you give tomorrow's social entrepreneurs? Be greedy for social change, and your life will be endlessly enriched. The only failure lies in not trying, or giving up.

What is the best piece of management advice you have received? Have faith in your intuition and listen to your gut feeling.

Source: "Leading questions," interview by Alison Benjamin, The Guardian

B Are these statements about the reading true (*T*), false (*F*), or is the information not given (*NG*) in the article? Write the correct letters.

_____ 1. A social entrepreneur works with people who struggle or have pain.

_____ 2. Ann Cotton used to work as a teacher.

_____ 3. Today, Camfed continues to raise money by selling homemade cakes.

_____ 4. Camfed's programs are run by the most highly trained experts in management.

_____ 5. Camfed's cause is girls' education and young women's leadership in Africa.

_____ 6. Ann Cotton's advice to young social entrepreneurs is to be greedy for money.

C **Group work** Discuss these questions in groups.

1. Do you think Ann Cotton is a very exceptional individual, or could any person have done what she did? Explain your answer.

2. Would you like to be a social entrepreneur? Why or why not?

LESSON A · Entrepreneurs

1. Success stories

starting point

A Match these descriptions of successful companies with the company name.

____ 1. The Body Shop   ____ 2. Google   ____ 3. Sanrio

Larry Page and Sergey Brin

a. Larry Page and Sergey Brin started this innovative company in a dorm room at Stanford University. They didn't get along at first, and had they been unable to work together, the most widely used Internet search engine might never have been created. Were you to ask about their company's goal, they'd smile and tell you it's to organize all of the world's information in order to make it accessible and useful.

b. Should you want to buy natural skin and hair care products, this company offers over 600 choices. Anita Roddick started the company to support her family. Were she to have been wealthy, she might not have gone into business. Her stores communicate a message about human rights and environmental issues. Her company is famous for its fair trade practices in impoverished communities.

Anita Roddick

Shintaro Tsuji

c. In 1960, Shintaro Tsuji created a line of character-branded lifestyle products centered around gift-giving occasions. However, had this Tokyo-based company not created Hello Kitty, it wouldn't have become nearly so successful. Hello Kitty goods are in demand all over the world. They include purses, wastebaskets, pads and pens, erasers, cell phone holders, and much, much more.

B **Pair work** Discuss these questions.

1. What might be some reasons for the success of these companies?

2. Can you think of other successful companies? What do they offer?

2. Business disasters

listening

A **Pair work** Brainstorm some of the factors that can make a business fail.

B Listen to two people discuss their unsuccessful businesses. What types of businesses did they start? Why did they choose those types? Complete the chart.

	Type of business	Reason for choosing it
1.		
2.		

C Listen again. Write the main reasons why each business failed.

1. _____

2. _____

3 Subject-verb inversion in conditional sentences

grammar

In past unreal conditional sentences, people sometimes replace *if* by inverting the subject and the auxiliary *had*. This occurs mainly in more formal speech and writing.
If they **had been** unable to work together, the search engine **might never have been** created.
Had they **been** unable to work together, the search engine **might never have been** created.

The same construction is possible for negative sentences. Notice that negative forms are not contracted and *not* is separated from *had* in these sentences.
If this company **hadn't created** Hello Kitty, it **wouldn't have become** nearly so successful.
Had this company **not created** Hello Kitty, it **wouldn't have become** nearly so successful.

In extremely formal situations, people often replace *if* by putting the past subjunctive *were* at the beginning of unreal conditional sentences.
Were she **to have been** wealthy, she **might not have gone** into business.

In present and future real conditionals, people often replace *if* by putting *should* at the beginning of the sentence. Note that this use of *should* does not express obligation.
Should you **want** to buy natural skin care products, this company offers over 600 choices.

Grammar Plus: See page 128.

A Look at the starting point on page 96 again. Can you find another conditional sentence with subject-verb inversion?

B Combine these pairs of sentences using conditional clauses and subject-verb inversion. Then compare with a partner. Sometimes more than one answer is possible.

1. That company didn't take the competition into consideration. It went out of business.

   Had that company taken the competition into consideration, it wouldn't have gone out of business.

2. That fast-food chain doesn't offer any healthy food options. Its sales are dropping.

3. Terry didn't develop a serious business plan. She missed a number of opportunities.

4. I decided to go to business school. I started my own business.

5. The government doesn't encourage international business. Its economy is slowing down.

6. My friends and I didn't know enough about the potential of the Internet. We didn't start an online business.

7. I knew it would take ten years to work off my college loans. I chose an affordable school.

8. I thought my friend would fail. I didn't loan her any money to start a business.

C **Pair work** Complete these sentences with your own information, and share them with a partner.

1. Had I saved more money when I was younger, . . .

2. Were all the students in the class to have started a small business, . . .

3. Had I not decided to take this English course, . . .

4. Had I followed my parents' advice, I would have . . .

5. Should I have the opportunity to start a business, I might . . .

6. Were I to discover a friend of mine was breaking the law, I'd probably . . .

4 Prepositions following *work*

vocabulary

A The expressions on the left are composed of *work* and a preposition. Match them with their definitions on the right.

1. work **against** progress ____
2. work **around** a problem ____
3. work **for** a boss ____
4. work **toward** a goal ____
5. work **off** a loan balance ____
6. work **on** a task ____

a. be employed by
b. apply effort to
c. work in order to prevent
d. work while avoiding (a difficulty)
e. work in order to achieve
f. work in order to eliminate

B Complete each statement with the correct preposition.

1. Entrepreneurs don't waste time trying to solve insolvable problems; they work _____ them.

2. Inexperience can work _____ young people looking for jobs.

3. Workers are happier when they work _____ a variety of projects, not just the same one.

4. Career training is expensive. It can take years to work _____ debt accumulated during college years.

5 Too good to be true?

discussion

A Read these advertising messages for different job opportunities. Are they believable? Make a comment about each one, either positive or negative.

❶ Break into the fashion industry! Our classes are your first step to working toward your goal of becoming a glamorous fashion model.

❷ Start your career in real estate. You can buy houses for as little as $2,000 and resell them for a huge profit with our real estate buying program.

❸ Do you have a computer and an Internet connection? Earn thousands every month just for surfing the Web!

❹ How would you like to get paid just for going shopping? Does it sound too good to be true? It's not. Ask us how!

❺ Invest like a professional. Send us $50 for information on how to make millions in the stock market.

Useful expressions

Expressing suspicion
That's a little hard to believe.
It sounds fishy to me.
It sounds too good to be true.

"The first one is a little hard to believe. I mean, I don't think you can become a fashion model just by taking classes – you have to be born with exceptionally good looks too."

B **Group work** Discuss the questions with your classmates.

1. Have you ever seen advertising messages like those above? Where?
2. What are some other examples of hard-to-believe advertisements?
3. Who do you think is attracted to these types of messages? Why?

6. Formal letters

writing

> Formal letters don't include personal information that is irrelevant to the topic. Unlike personal letters, formal letters tend to avoid contractions and idioms.

A Read this formal letter and then label the five parts listed in the box.

> **1.** The heading includes your address and the date. It typically goes in the top left corner. If you use letterhead stationery with an address, only the date is added.
>
> **2.** The inside address is below the heading. It contains the addressee's name, title (if you know it), and address.
>
> **3.** For the greeting, you should write "Dear" and "Mr." or "Ms." along with the person's family name. If you don't have a specific person to contact, write "Dear Sir or Madam." The greeting is usually followed by a colon (:).
>
> **4.** The body of the letter follows. The first paragraph is used to state the reason for the letter. The paragraphs that follow should each focus on only one point. The letter generally concludes by thanking the reader in some way.
>
> **5.** The closing includes a closing phrase, your signature, and your name and title.

1 ——

35 Henry St.
New York, NY 10002

July 10, 2008

→DM←

Mr. Jonathan Hayes, Director
Institute for Study Abroad
1472 Park Avenue
Summit, NJ 07091

Dear Mr. Hayes:

I am writing to request more information concerning your study abroad programs. Your programs sound extremely interesting to me, and I hope to participate in one of them next year. Your Study Abroad in Paris program sounds particularly fascinating.

I would like to sign up for the Paris program beginning in June. I'm still trying to decide whether to choose the homestay option or the dormitory option. Would it be possible to send me further information about those two choices in order to help me make a decision?

I realize that all the spaces in your Paris program may already be filled. In that case, my second choice would be the Study Abroad in Toulouse program. My third choice would be your Study Abroad in Strasbourg program.

Thank you very much for your help. I look forward to receiving the information.

Sincerely,

Donna Malnick

Donna Malnick

B Imagine that you are interested in learning more about a job or program. Write your formal letter to the program director expressing interest and requesting information. Include all five parts of a formal letter.

1 Attitudes at work

starting point

A What kinds of working conditions would you like at your job? Check (✓) the statements you agree with.

What are you looking for in a job?

1. I would be happier and more productive if my workspace were neat and organized.

2. I would take almost any job provided that there were opportunities to learn.

3. I wouldn't care about a high salary if a job allowed me to balance my work, family, and social life.

4. I wouldn't mind working in an office, assuming that I had the freedom to be creative.

5. If the company I worked for dealt fairly with me, I would be loyal to it.

6. I would only take a job on the condition that it offered long-term security.

7. I would quit a job that required me to be dishonest, whether or not it were high paying.

8. Supposing I had the choice, I would prefer to work with a group rather than by myself.

B **Group work** Compare your answers with the members of your group. How are you different? Do you think you would make a harmonious group of co-workers?

2 The dream job

discussion

A **Pair work** Look at this checklist of considerations in choosing a job. Add two more items to the list. Then check (✓) the three items that are the most important to you.

The ideal job . . .

- [ ] allows me to travel often.
- [ ] offers me a high salary.
- [ ] isn't stressful at all.
- [ ] doesn't require long hours.
- [ ] gives me the freedom to be creative.
- [ ] has a flexible schedule.
- [ ] lets me wear casual clothes.
- [ ] has an excellent health plan and benefits.
- [ ] has lots of opportunity for advancement.
- [ ] is close to my home or school.
- [ ] _____
- [ ] _____

B **Group work** Join another pair to compare and explain your choices.

"I think the ideal job should have a flexible schedule."

"I guess so, but I think a high salary is more important than that."

3 Adverb clauses of condition

grammar

Conditional sentences do not necessarily use *if*. The following expressions are also used. The tense agreement in the clauses is the same as in conditional sentences with *if*.

Provided (that) and *on the condition (that)* introduce a condition on which another situation depends.
I would take almost any job **provided that** there were opportunities to learn.
I would only take a job **on the condition that** it offered long-term security.

Whether or not introduces a condition that does not influence another situation.
I would quit a job that required me to be dishonest, **whether or not** it were high paying.

Assuming (that) introduces an assumption upon which another condition depends.
I wouldn't mind working in an office, **assuming that** I had the freedom to be creative.

Supposing (that) introduces a possible condition that could influence another situation.
Supposing I had the choice, I would prefer to work with a group rather than by myself.

Grammar Plus: See page 129.

A Look at the starting point on page 100 again. Can you replace the sentences with *if* with another expression?

B Match the items to make logical sentences.

1. Whether or not you have a clear job description, ____
2. Assuming that you have an original idea, ____
3. On the condition that I didn't have to be away for more than two or three days, ____
4. Provided that I could find extra time, ____
5. Supposing a close friend wanted to start a business with you, ____

a. you might be able to start a business.
b. I would be willing to travel on business.
c. would you jump at the opportunity?
d. I'd like to do some volunteer work.
e. you need to be flexible and cooperative.

C **Pair work** Complete these sentences with your own information. Then discuss them with a partner.

1. I would enjoy managing an office, assuming . . .
   I had responsible people working for me.
2. Provided a company paid for my commute, I . . .
3. Whether or not I have enough money in the bank, I . . .
4. I would take a reduction in salary on the condition that . . .
5. Supposing that I couldn't find a job, I . . .
6. I would agree to work overtime, assuming that . . .
7. On the condition that I were guaranteed two weeks' vacation a year, . . .

4 Qualities essential for success

vocabulary & speaking

A Choose three qualities that are important to working alone successfully and three that are important to working with others. Write them in the chart.

A SUCCESSFUL WORKER NEEDS TO . . . .

- have good communication skills
- have initiative
- have self-discipline
- be trustworthy
- be innovative
- have leadership ability
- be adaptable
- have influence
- be optimistic
- have charisma
- be conscientious
- have specialized training

To work alone successfully, you need to	To work well with others, you need to . . . .
have initiative	

B Pair work Discuss the qualities you chose. Why do you think they're important?

"I feel you can work alone successfully, provided you have initiative."

"I totally agree. You need to have a lot of initiative because you don't have a boss to tell you what to do."

5 Can you really learn that?

listening

A Listen to three people who participated in workshops for their jobs. What type of workshop did each person attend?

1. Anne: _____ 2. Thomas: _____ 3. Paulina: _____

B Listen again. What did each person learn from their workshop experience?

Anne: _____

Thomas: _____

Paulina: _____

C Pair work Would you like to take part in such a workshop? Why or why not? Discuss your reasons.

Working with others

reading

A **Pair work** Do your friends have similar values and temperaments? Read the article and make a list of three categories that your friends would fit into.

The Value of Difference

Every person is unique. We work with many people who are different from us. It is important to realize that differences are good and to appreciate that not all people are like us. On a team, the strengths of one worker can overcome the weaknesses of another. The balance created by such variety makes a team stronger.

There are three basic ways that people differ from one another: values, temperament, and individual diversity (gender, age, etc.).

One major difference among workers is personal values. Values are the importance that we give to ideas, things, or people. While our values may be quite different, organizational behavior expert Stephen Robbins suggests that people fall into one of three general categories:

Traditionalists. People in this category value hard work, doing things the way they've always been done, loyalty to the organization, and the authority of leaders.

Humanists. People in this category value quality of life, autonomy, loyalty to self, and leaders who are attentive to workers' needs.

Pragmatists. People in this category value success, achievement, loyalty to career, and leaders who reward people for hard work.

Another important way in which people differ is temperament. Your temperament is the distinctive way you think, feel, and react to the world. All of us have our own individual temperaments. However, experts have found that it is easier to understand the differences in temperament by classifying people into four categories:

Optimists. People with this temperament must be free and not tied down. They're impulsive, they enjoy the immediate, and they like working with things. The optimist is generous and cheerful and enjoys action for action's sake.

Realists. People with this temperament like to belong to groups. They have a strong sense of obligation and are committed to society's standards. The realist is serious, likes order, and finds traditions important.

Pragmatists. People with this temperament like to control things and want to be competitive. The pragmatist is self-critical, strives for excellence, focuses on the future, and is highly creative.

Idealists. People with this temperament want to know the meaning of things. They appreciate others and get along well with people of all temperaments. The idealist is romantic, writes fluently, and values integrity.

Source: "Job Savvy: How to Be a Success at Work," by LaVerne Ludden

B Match the categories from the article with the descriptions.

1. traditionalist ____   a. generous and cheerful; enjoys action for action's sake
2. humanist ____   b. serious and likes order; has a strong sense of obligation
3. optimist ____   c. values quality of life; attentive to workers' needs
4. realist ____   d. strives for excellence; focuses on the future
5. pragmatist ____   e. values doing things the way they've always been done
6. idealist ____   f. romantic; writes fluently; values integrity

C **Group work** Discuss these questions. Then share your answers with the class.

1. How would you categorize your own values and temperament?

2. Which category of people would you prefer to work with? Why?

Communication review

Self-assessment

How well can you do these things? Rate your ability from 1 to 5 (1 = low, 5 = high).

Give advice to people using adverb clauses of condition (Ex. 1)	_____
Listen to a lecture using superlative compound adjectives, adverb clauses of condition, and discourse markers (Ex. 2)	_____
Listen to and recognize subject-verb agreement with quantifiers (Ex. 2)	_____
Discuss personal qualities using superlative adjectives (Ex. 3)	_____
Talk about personality traits using character adjectives (Ex. 4)	_____

Now do the corresponding exercises below. Were your ratings correct?

1 Speaking tips

speaking

A Pair work What would each person have to do to succeed? Think of several conditions that would work for each situation.

1. Renata has been asked to give a formal talk on a topic she knows little about.
2. Johana has been asked to give a short speech at a friend's wedding.
3. Hal is too timid to join in the group's conversation after class.
4. Wei-pin had some bad experiences at job interviews, and now he gets really nervous before them.

B Group work Discuss your ideas with another pair. Do you have similar suggestions?

"Providing Renata spends time reading about the topic, she shouldn't have a problem."

"That's true, assuming she has time to do plenty of research and rehearse the talk."

2 Good language learners

listening

A Listen to a lecture about good language learning. Who is the lecture for? Check (✓) the correct answer.

☐ a. language learners   ☐ b. tourists   ☐ c. language teachers

B Listen again. Check (✓) the compound adjectives that are used to describe good language learners.

☐ 1. highly motivated   ☐ 4. pattern-seeking   ☐ 7. well-known

☐ 2. forward-thinking   ☐ 5. open-minded   ☐ 8. self-aware

☐ 3. risk-taking   ☐ 6. well-organized   ☐ 9. widely recognized

3. Superlative compound adjectives

discussion

A Complete the sentences with your own information. Add reasons for your opinions, and compare with a partner.

1. The most open-minded person in my family is . . .
2. Of all the people I know, the most hardworking is . . .
3. The most widely respected person I've ever met is . . .
4. One of the best-looking people I've ever seen is . . .
5. The most easygoing person I've ever worked with is . . .
6. The most well-read person I've ever met is . . .

"My sister Suzanne is the most open-minded person in our family. She's always willing to go to new places and try new things."

B **Pair work** Who are some people you both admire? Use the superlative form of these compound adjectives to write sentences about them. Give reasons.

1. good-looking   2. thought-provoking   3. widely respected   4. kind-hearted

4. Personal qualities

speaking

A Which of these people is most similar to you, and which is least similar?

Roberta

❝ *I've been told that I'm a charismatic person. The truth is that I'm a people person, and I'm not afraid to share my ideas with others.* ❞

Li-cho

❝ *I'm very optimistic. I try to look at the good side of things, and I'm always confident that even the worst situations will turn out to be fine.* ❞

Alberto

❝ *I've lived in three different countries and have attended six different schools. Yet I've never had problems adapting to new situations.* ❞

B **Pair work** Which of these are your strongest qualities? Which do you feel are most necessary to realize your own personal and professional goals?

- adaptability
- charisma
- conscientiousness
- determination
- honesty
- initiative
- optimism
- self-confidence
- self-control

"I think I'm very adaptable. Since I'd like to be an actor, and the work is unpredictable, I think it's an important quality."

Grammar Plus

Additional phrasal verbs
Separable: call off, count out, cut off, get across, hand over, pass up, see through, take back
Inseparable: go over, hang around, live up to, look after, pick on, run out of, touch on
Intransitive: catch on, come along, come over, fall apart, show up, turn out

Certain intransitive two-word phrasal verbs, when followed by a preposition, can then take an object.

back down (from)	cut back (on)	drop out (of)	give in (to)
catch up (to)	cut down (on)	get along (with)	give up (on)
check out (of)	drop in (on)	get away (with)	look back (on)

When confronted with an argument, Mark never **backs down**.
Mark never **backs down from** an argument.

1 Underline the phrasal verb in each sentence. Is the verb separable (*S*) or inseparable (*I*)? Is it transitive (*T*) or intransitive (*NT*)? Write the correct letters.

<u>S, T</u> 1. The referees <u>called</u> the soccer match <u>off</u> due to heavy rain.

_____ 2. Jessica asked me to come over to her house for dinner.

_____ 3. Sometimes I find it hard to live up to my parents' expectations.

_____ 4. Sally insulted me yesterday, but today she took back her remark.

_____ 5. When entertaining, there's nothing worse than running out of food at your party.

_____ 6. When Mark gave me the chance to share his apartment, I couldn't pass up the opportunity.

2 Complete the sentences with intransitive phrasal verbs and a preposition from the grammar box above. Be sure to use the correct form of the verb.

1. When my grandfather and I go jogging together, I sometimes need to stop and wait for him to __catch up to__ me.

2. I didn't want to try bungee jumping, but I finally _____ the pressure from my friends and tried it. It was fun!

3. Even when you fail, a true friend will never _____ you.

4. My friends and I are trying to _____ the money we spend, so on Fridays we just watch TV at my house.

5. Mia's father is successful, even though he _____ college.

6. There's a long line of people waiting to _____ the hotel.

7. I insist on honesty; I won't let anyone _____ lying to me.

1B Gerund and infinitive constructions

The verbs *forget, mean,* and *regret* can be followed by either an infinitive or a gerund. However, the meaning is significantly different in each case.

Forget followed by an infinitive refers to something you didn't actually do. *Forget* followed by a gerund refers to an action that you in fact did earlier.
Marcello **forgot to meet** his best friend at the train station.
Marcello never **forgot meeting** his favorite actor.

Mean followed by an infinitive means "intend." In this case, *mean* is usually used in the negative or in the past tense. *Mean* followed by a gerund means "involve or necessitate."
I **meant to visit** Sheila while I was in Hawaii, but I didn't have the chance.
Inviting Emile to the party **means inviting** Eva too. She'd be so insulted if we didn't.

Regret followed by infinitives such as *inform, announce,* and *say* is a polite way of introducing bad news in official communication. *Regret* followed by a gerund means "be sorry for / about."
The corporation **regrets to inform** you that all job vacancies have been filled.
Donna really **regretted missing** her best friend's wedding.

Be + adjective expressions are often followed by an infinitive.

be amazed	be determined	be happy	be lucky
be ashamed	be eager	be hesitant	be ready

Many verb + preposition / adjective expressions are followed by a gerund.

apologize for	complain about	object to	take part in	be used to
be bored with	be convinced of	participate in	think of	be worried about

1 Circle the correct form of the verb.

1. Manny forgot *to do* / (*doing*) his homework for English class because he completed it over a month ago.

2. Mina didn't mean *to frighten* / *frightening* the baby with the doll.

3. Though she didn't have much, Wen never regretted *to spend* / *spending* money on her friends.

4. I always forget *to call* / *calling* my parents, and they get really mad at me.

5. Attending my high school reunion means *to meet* / *meeting* old friends as well as people I didn't like very much.

6. We regret *to announce* / *announcing* that Flight 54 has been delayed.

2 Complete the sentences with the infinitive or gerund form of the verb in parentheses.

1. Mark is really eager __to rekindle__ his relationship with Lana. (rekindle)

2. I would like to apologize for _____ all these old issues. (rehash)

3. I think you're really lucky _____ so many close friends. (have)

4. Have you thought of _____ an e-card instead of mailing a card? (send)

5. I'm ashamed _____ that my college roommate and I never reconnected. (say)

6. I've been worried about _____ my new college roommate. (meet)

Here are some verbs that are used with each pattern.

a. verb + infinitive
afford, fail, hasten, learn, prepare, proceed, seek, strive
I really **strive to wear** the latest styles and trends.

b. verb + object + infinitive
advise, allow, authorize, cause, convince, encourage, instruct, permit, persuade, urge
The salesperson **convinced me to buy** a dress I knew I didn't need.

c. verb + gerund
can't help, can't see, can't stand, enjoy, get through, keep on, (not) mind, miss, postpone, risk
I **can't see paying** high prices for clothes that will be out of style in a year.

d. verb + object + preposition + gerund/noun
blame (for), dissuade (from), forgive (for), interest (in), keep (from), suspect (of), thank (for)
Can I **interest you in going** on a shopping spree with me?

1 Label the words in boldface with the correct verb pattern above.

A famous saying goes, "Clothes make the man." My mother used to say that to me because I was a sloppy dresser, and she (1) _b_ **urged me to look** my best. She'd coax me to dress better, but nothing could (2) ___ **keep me from wearing** jeans. At my high school, students never (3) ___ **failed to wear** jeans to school, and my mother always sighed and tried to (4) ___ **dissuade me from leaving** the house in my old, torn jeans. On my graduation from high school, my parents gave me my first suit and (5) ___ **advised me to "dress** for success."

Since then, I've changed quite a bit. I really (6) ___ **enjoy dressing** fashionably. I can (7) ___ **afford to wear** stylish slacks and silk shirts, with well-polished shoes. It's funny, but I (8) ___ **don't miss wearing** jeans one bit.

2 Complete the sentences by putting the words in parentheses in the correct order and by choosing the correct verb form. Which pattern does each sentence follow?

_d_ 1. I _forgave my sister for spilling_ ketchup on my blouse. (my sister / forgive / spill / for)

___ 2. I never _____ a birthday present for my brother. (mind / buy)

___ 3. Harold _____ his jacket. (allow / wear / me)

___ 4. Shirley _____ her dry cleaning for another week. (pick up / postpone)

___ 5. Lydia's dad _____ him a necktie for Father's Day. (get / her / thank / for)

___ 6. The man stole the sneakers, then _____ them around the store. (wear / proceeded)

To emphasize the whole sentence rather than just the part following the main verb, use a cleft sentence with *what* and a form of the verb *do*.

I try to project a positive attitude.
What I try to project is a positive attitude. (emphasizes *a positive attitude*)
What I do is try to project a positive attitude. (emphasizes whole sentence)

She complained to the waiter about the quality of the food.
What she complained about to the waiter was the quality of the food.
What she did was complain to the waiter about the quality of the food.

Cleft structures can include expressions like *the reason why, the thing that, the place where,* and *the person who*. These structures are typically used with the verb *be*.
I'm wearing sunglasses to protect my eyes.
The reason why I'm wearing sunglasses **is** to protect my eyes.

I do all my shopping at the mall.
The place where I do all my shopping **is** (at) the mall.

1 Rewrite these sentences as cleft sentences with *what* to emphasize the whole sentence.

1. The candidate showed the voters he was a trustworthy man.
   What the candidate did was show the voters he was a trustworthy man.

2. My mother shouldn't have made me wear my sister's old clothes.

3. I'm going to send all my shirts out to be dry cleaned.

4. My friends call me at work all the time.

5. My father judges people too much by their appearance.

6. Employees should carry ID cards at all times.

7. Eleanor wore her mother's wedding dress at her own wedding.

8. Martin spilled spaghetti sauce on his shirt.

9. Sam bought a whole new wardrobe.

10. Mary is going to wear her diamond necklace to the party.

2 Rewrite these sentences as cleft sentences by starting them with the expressions in parentheses.

1. I'm wearing a tie to impress my boss. (the reason why)
   The reason why I'm wearing a tie is to impress my boss.

2. I lost my watch in the park. (the place where)

3. The office dress code changed last Friday. (the day when)

4. My dog wears a sweater because his fur is short. (the reason why)

5. I remember the intense expression on his face. (the thing that)

6. Mami keeps her jewelry under her bed. (the place where)

3A Indefinite and definite articles

In completely general statements with uncountable nouns, do not use an article before the noun. However, *the* is required when the noun is made more specific by a modifying phrase following the noun.

Ethics are becoming an important part of the field of genetics.
The ethics of cloning need to be addressed by experts in the field.

Image is an important part of success.
The image she projected did not serve her well in court.

With certain exceptions, do not use *the* before:
countries (exceptions: the Netherlands, the Philippines, the United Kingdom, the United States)
cities and streets (exception: The Hague)
individual lakes, bays, islands, mountain peaks, continents (exception: the Matterhorn)

Do use *the* before:
rivers, oceans, seas, gulfs, mountain ranges, peninsulas, deserts, forests

1 Do the nouns in these sentences require a definite article? Write *the*, or ✗ if none is needed.

1. A large number of oil wells have been drilled in __the__ Gulf of Mexico.
2. There is no room for _____ frivolity when discussing _____ safety of nuclear power.
3. _____ United States utilizes more genetically modified food than _____ Europe does.
4. On an insecure Internet connection, _____ confidentiality can never be guaranteed.
5. Thanks to our GPS system, we know that the car is located on _____ Elm Street.
6. There are many people who do not believe that _____ rights of animals should be protected.
7. A global warming monitoring station is located on top of _____ Mount Rutherford.
8. _____ Carelessness is the cause of many problems in nuclear power plants.

2 Review the rules for articles on page 19. Then fill in the blanks with a definite article, an indefinite article, or ✗ if none is needed.

(1) __✗__ Energy seems to be on everyone's mind these days. (2) _____ People are worried because they know that petroleum reserves are not infinite. It's also alarming that (3) _____ temperature of the earth seems to be rising year by year. Many scientists blame (4) _____ warming of the earth on (5) _____ burning of petroleum-based fuels. However, there is no reason to give up (6) _____ hope, as (7) _____ alternatives are available. (8) _____ wind farm is a collection of windmills that turn wind energy into electric power. (9) _____ Hydroelectric facilities are able to change (10) _____ energy created by moving water into electric power; (11) _____ world's largest hydroelectric facility is located on (12) _____ Paraná River in Brazil. (13) _____ Solar power is (14) _____ clean source of energy that is attracting (15) _____ attention as well. Several countries, including (16) _____ Australia, (17) _____ Germany, and (18) _____ China have announced plans to build large solar power plants. Lastly, it's important that we all conserve energy. Take (19) _____ moment to shut off and unplug any electrical items when you leave (20) _____ room.

3B -ing clauses

When *-ing* clauses begin a sentence, the agent of the *-ing* clause must be the subject of the main clause that follows.

Incorrect: Trying hard to fix my computer, ~~the dog~~ kept staring at me.
(The agent of the *-ing* clause seems to be *the dog*.)
Correct: Trying hard to fix my computer, **I** noticed the dog staring at me.
(The agent of the *-ing* clause and the subject of the main clause are the same.)

Incorrect: Changing the oil in my car, ~~my hands~~ got very dirty.
(The agent of the *-ing* clause seems to be *my hands*.)
Correct: Changing the oil in my car, **I** got dirt all over my hands.
(The agent of the *-ing* clause and the subject of the main clause are the same.)

In addition to starting a sentence, *-ing* clauses can also follow these expressions:

have a good time	have an easy time	have fun	spend time
have a hard time	have difficulty	have problems	waste time

1 Choose the correct main clause that makes sense with the *-ing* clause.

1. Making strange noises, __b__
   a. I knew that my computer would crash.
   b. my computer stopped working.

2. Being technophiles, ____
   a. we subscribe to technology magazines.
   b. new technology always interests us.

3. Talking on her cell phone, ____
   a. the car went right through a red light.
   b. Pam didn't pay attention to her driving.

4. Traveling by horse and buggy, ____
   a. the Amish reject the modern convenience of cars.
   b. the convenience of cars is rejected by the Amish.

2 Combine these sentences using an expression from the grammar box above to start the sentence.

1. I played video games all day Saturday. I had a good time.
   I had a good time playing video games all day Saturday.

2. My brother was shopping for cars. He had a hard time.

3. Fred surfs the Web all day. He wastes a lot of time.

4. I'm attending the big technology expo next week. I'm going to have fun.

5. Nash is having difficulty. He's trying to comprehend the concept of artificial intelligence.

6. Norah was writing a genetic technology lecture. She spent a lot of time on it.

7. The guard used the video surveillance camera to identify the intruder. He had an easy time.

4A Reporting clauses

In reporting clauses, verbs such as *admit, agree, announce, comment, complain, confess, disclose, explain, inform,* and *reveal* are frequently followed by an indirect object. In this case, *that* should be retained for clarity.

Several people agreed **with me that** logic, not superstition, is the best way to make decisions.
Max explained **to the teacher that** a black cat never means bad luck in his country.

The following nouns are also often used in reporting clauses. Here, too, *that* is helpful in making the meaning clear and should be retained.

accusation	assertion	comment	explanation	response
argument	claim	decision	remark	suggestion

Bill made the **assertion that** he'd have no luck at all if it weren't for bad luck.
Liliana repeated her **argument that** only foolish people believe in magic.
The class rejected Niran's **suggestion that** we cancel class on Friday the thirteenth.

1 Using the words in parentheses, rewrite these sentences with reporting clauses.

1. He had an irrational fear of spiders. (Luis / admit / his friend)
   Luis admitted to his friend that he had an irrational fear of spiders.

2. Some people really are luckier than others. (Min / agree / me)

3. There are too many pigeons in the park. (many people / complain / park staff)

4. He had spent his father's lucky dollar on candy. (Marco / confess / his mother)

5. It's bad luck to step on a crack in the sidewalk. (Marcie / explain / her little sister)

6. The day he met his wife was the luckiest day of his life. (Felix / announce / his wedding guests)

2 Combine the sentences using a reporting clause with one of the nouns from the grammar box above.

1. Kim accused Anna of being a superstitious person. Anna didn't agree.
   Anna didn't agree with Kim's accusation that she was a superstitious person.

2. Gianna argues that everything happens for a reason. Many people disagree.

3. Leslie asserted that all superstition is based in fear. Carlos didn't understand.

4. Jae Woo decided that a trip to Las Vegas was what he needed. His friends were surprised.

5. Ernesto commented that hard work is more important than luck. Lily repeated what he said.

6. Hiroshi claimed he had won the chess game thanks to beginner's luck. Sandra didn't believe him.

7. Patrick remarked that Tanya probably shouldn't push her luck. Tanya ignored what he said.

8. Mr. Wang responded that actions speak louder than words. I understood him.

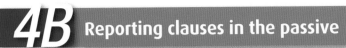

4B Reporting clauses in the passive

The following verbs can be used in reporting clauses in the passive.

announce   deny   maintain   reveal   suggest
confirm   estimate   observe   rumor   understand

Reporting clauses in the passive are commonly used with a variety of structures.
Simple present: It **is suggested** that passengers report anything suspicious to the driver.
Simple past: It **was** flatly **denied** that any government radar station had sighted a UFO.
Present perfect: It **has been estimated** that over half of all Americans believe in UFOs.
Past perfect: It **had been rumored** that a monster was living in the lake.
With modals: It **couldn't be denied** that many mysteries elude scientific understanding.
With past modals: It **should have been confirmed** that the flight would be delayed.

Reporting clauses in the passive are used in written and formal English and are not common in conversation.

1   Add a reporting clause in the passive with *it* to these statements. Use the verb and the suggested structure.

1. The lost city of Atlantis had been discovered on April Fool's Day, 1980. (announce, simple past)

   It was announced that the lost city of Atlantis had been discovered on April Fool's Day, 1980.

2. Human beings have 30,000 to 40,000 genes. (reveal, present perfect)

3. Some people have a higher level of intuition than others. (understand, simple present)

4. Crop circles, patterns created by flattening crops, are a clever hoax. (can't deny, modal)

5. The moon's pull on the earth affects the ocean tides. (maintain, simple present)

6. The politician was deceiving the nation. (should reveal, past modal)

7. A positive attitude was an important part of his cure. (observe, simple past)

8. The completed Great Pyramid contained 2,300,000 blocks of stone. (estimate, past perfect)

2   Rewrite these statements with a reporting clause in the passive with *it*.

1. An unknown source maintains that the Loch Ness Monster has been sighted again.

   It is maintained that the Loch Ness Monster has been sighted again.

2. A group of people have revealed that the first images of a giant squid have been filmed.

3. Officials should have observed that there was a mysterious substance on the train floor.

4. People can't deny that ancient civilizations possessed knowledge lost to us today.

5. People have spread rumors that another monster was found in Siberia.

6. The authorities have announced that ten people on the ship got ill.

5A Such ... that and so ... that

In written English, *so* and *such* are most often followed by a *that* clause. However, in conversation, the *that* clause is frequently omitted and gives *so* or *such* emphatic stress.

The host on that game show is **so** funny!

That actress plays her role **so** convincingly!

The writers of that new sitcom show **such** originality!

That was **such** a great documentary!

So much, *so little*, *so many*, and *so few* can also be used without a *that* clause and for emphatic stress.

There are **so many** reality TV shows these days!

That quiz show gives away **so much** money!

In conversation, *much* and *little* can be used as adverbs following *so*.

Why do you watch TV **so much**? (*much = frequently*)

That actor is featured **so little** that I sometimes forget he's on the show. (*little = infrequently*)

Much, *little*, *many*, and *few* can also serve as pronouns for nouns.

TV can be bad for your health. I sometimes watch so **much** (TV) my eyes hurt.

He needs to earn more money. He makes so **little** (money) he can't afford his cable TV bill.

I don't watch soap operas anymore. I've seen so **many** (soap operas) that I'm tired of them.

Educational shows are good for children, but there are so **few** (educational shows) that I won't let my kids watch TV.

1 Complete these sentences with *so*, *such*, *so much*, *so little*, *so many*, or *so few*.

1. You should have seen the new World War II documentary. It was
   _____so_____ interesting!

2. I don't want cable TV. What would I do with _____ channels?

3. Why do you kids spend _____ time in front of the TV? It's not healthy!

4. Turn off that program right now! I've never heard _____ language!

5. I think travel programs are _____ fascinating!

6. Shelby works long hours. He has _____ time for TV.

2 Fill in the blanks with *so*, *such*, *so much*, *so little*, *so many*, or *so few*.

Television can be (1) _____such_____ a wonderful source of education and information for children. Unfortunately, many sit in front of the "tube" (2) _____ that they become overweight. What about exercise? Some children get (3) _____ that their muscles don't develop properly. Children also need to be guided away from programs with violence or adult themes. There are (4) _____ nowadays that a channel-surfing child is sure to come across one. As far as educational programs aimed at children, there are (5) _____ that we need to ask TV stations to offer more choices. But, as you know, it's all about money. TV networks make (6) _____ that they don't feel the need to change their ways. Where is their sense of social responsibility? They seem to have (7) _____ that they put profit over our children's well-being. It just makes me (8) _____ angry!

5B Sentence adverbs

To express the speaker's attitude about the entire sentence, sentence adverbs are most often located at the beginning of the sentence and set off by a comma.
Predictably, the hero of the novel won the heart of the girl.

Sentence adverbs can be used in place of longer clauses that modify a sentence.
People were amazed that Tom was able to write his first novel in one week.
Amazingly, Tom was able to write his first novel in one week.

Nobody was surprised that Tom's first novel didn't sell well.
Not surprisingly, Tom's first novel didn't sell well.

The following conjunctive adverbs link a sentence with a preceding idea.
accordingly   consequently   hence   indeed   meanwhile   otherwise   thus

The poet took the stage to begin his reading; **accordingly,** the audience took their seats and fell silent.

1 Rewrite the sentences using sentence adverbs to replace the boldfaced words.

1. **It's apparent to me that** clichéd stories are still very popular.

   Apparently, clichéd stories are still very popular.

2. **It's fortunate that** I remembered my book for the 13-hour plane ride.

3. **I'm being honest when I say that** I just don't care for love stories, no matter how moving they may be.

4. **Nobody can question the fact that** many historical novels present an incorrect view of history.

5. **It was bad luck that** Carol lost that novel just before she finished it.

6. **In essence,** the novel is a tale of good versus evil.

7. **If it fulfills its potential,** the Internet could increase literacy rates.

8. **It's obvious to me that** you are only pretending to have read the book.

9. **I'm being serious when I say that** I would rather buy books than clothes.

2 Complete the sentences with a conjunctive adverb from the grammar box above. Sometimes more than one answer is possible.

1. I never read very much in high school. <u>Consequently</u> , it was difficult for me to manage all the reading I had to do in college.

2. Craig was reading the article to us. _____ , Samantha was trying to get our attention.

3. I have trouble reading because I'm dyslexic; _____ , I listen to a lot of audio books.

4. I used to read a great deal, but I recently had a baby; _____ , I don't have much time to read anymore.

5. You need to pre-order the book; _____ , you'll never get a copy on time.

6. I knew I recognized the movie's story line. _____ , it was based on a book I read last year.

6A Double comparatives

These structures are commonly used in double comparatives.

The + more / less + clause
The more I listen to classical music, the more I appreciate it.

The + comparative form of adjective + clause
The more romantic a song is, the less my brother wants to listen to it.

The + comparative form of adverb + clause
The louder Mario plays his stereo, the more his neighbors complain.

The + more / less / fewer + noun/gerund + clause
The more dancing you do, the more natural you'll feel on the dance floor.

Short double comparatives without verbs are common in conversation. Many of them end in **the better**.
The more, the merrier!
The bigger, the better!
The sooner, the better!

1 Fill in the blanks to create appropriate double comparatives. For comparatives with adjectives or adverbs, more than one answer is possible.

1. Ricky seems to play his music loud in his car in order to get attention. __The louder__ the music is, __the more__ people turn their heads.

2. This CD is so catchy! _____ I listen, _____ I like it.

3. The price of concert tickets has really gone up. And, _____ the performer is, _____ the ticket is.

4. I love soothing background music. _____ the music is, _____ stress it removes from my body and mind.

5. They play music at the baseball game to get the fans excited. _____ the music plays, _____ the fans yell.

6. It's true that practice makes perfect. _____ you practice, _____ you will become.

7. Even age won't slow that performer down. _____ she gets, _____ performances she gives.

2 Fill in the blanks with an appropriate short double comparative without verbs from the grammar box above.

1. A: When should we officially end this meeting?
   B: _____ !

2. A: How many people do you think we should invite to the party?
   B: _____ !

3. A: What would you like your new house to be like?
   B: _____ !

6B *Will* and *would* for habits and general truths

Used to and *would* are both used to express habits in the past.
Before he became a big star, Mark **used to** play music on the street for money.
Before he became a big star, Mark **would** play music on the street for money.

However, *would* cannot be used with stative verbs such as *be, have, like, live, love, mean,* and *own.*
Correct: When I was young, I **used to** have a clarinet.
Incorrect: When I was young, I ~~would~~ have a clarinet.

1 Complete the sentences using *would* wherever possible. If *would* is not possible, use *used to.*

1. Before he made it big, Elvis _____would_____ listen to blues and gospel music on the porch of his family home in Mississippi.

2. I _____ own a cheap violin that my uncle gave me for my birthday. I don't know where it is now.

3. Since the young Beethoven loved nature, he _____ take long walks along the banks of the river Rhine.

4. That performer _____ be washed up, but he has since made a remarkable comeback.

5. Before he was discovered by a Hollywood talent scout, that singer _____ regularly announce local sports events on the radio.

6. Some people claim that John Lennon _____ like to fish from the window of his room when he stayed at Seattle's Edgewater Hotel.

7. In the 1990s, Pavarotti _____ perform as part of the Three Tenors with José Carreras and Plácido Domingo.

8. In high school, Madonna _____ love to dance and _____ always get perfect grades.

9. Although my family wasn't wealthy, we _____ own a concert-quality grand piano.

2 Complete the paragraph using the correct form of the verb in parentheses. Use *would* or *will* for habits and general truths wherever possible.

Music has played an important role in my life since I was very young. When I was a boy, in the center of the small town where I grew up, our family (1) ____would sit____ (sit) on the green lawn on Saturday nights listening to the town band. Between songs, I (2) _____ (like) to talk to the musicians about their instruments, which fascinated me. I (3) _____ (ask) them if I could play their trumpets and clarinets, and they (4) _____ (say) no in as gentle a way as they could. Who could have imagined that I would become an instrument maker? I've got my own family now. On warm Saturdays, I (5) _____ (take) them down to the center of town to listen to the town band. And, every time we go, my own son (6) _____ (bother) the musicians with questions and requests. After all, like father, like son!

7A Optional and required relative pronouns

When the relative pronoun is the complement (or object) of a preposition, *whom* is required (not *who*).
Hunting whales is illegal for everyone except indigenous people **to whom** special hunting permits have been issued.

Similarly, *which* is required (not *that*) when the preposition precedes the relative pronoun.
My parents' generation stood for certain principles **against which** my generation has rebelled.

The relative pronoun *whose* is not only used for people. It can also represent animals or things. This relative pronoun is required.
Today there are many widely used prescription drugs **whose** dangers have become evident only after many years of use.

1 Complete the sentences with *whom, which,* or *whose.*

1. Junk food advertisements are particularly effective in influencing the buying patterns of the youths to _____whom_____ they are aimed.

2. "Where is society heading?" is a difficult question, the answer to _____ I don't think anybody really knows.

3. The government currently offers low-cost health insurance to people _____ workplace doesn't offer any.

4. I'd like to join the debate about the future of international travel, but I'm afraid it's a subject about _____ I know almost nothing.

5. Improper or insufficient education is the root of intolerance. The world would change for the better if we really understood the people against _____ we have illogical prejudices.

6. My parents owned a fully detached house with a big yard. Unfortunately, my friends and I are all apartment dwellers for _____ owning such a house just isn't possible.

2 Review the rules for pronouns on page 55. Fill in the blanks with an appropriate relative pronoun. Sometimes more than one answer is possible.

I once read a story about a little boy (1) _____who_____ received an insect – a large beetle – for his birthday. Frustrated by the insect's frantic movements, the boy turned it over and over looking for a switch (2) _____ could turn it off. Clearly, this was a boy (3) _____ understanding of animals and the natural world was extremely limited. The result was a boy for (4) _____ a living thing was indistinguishable from a toy. Parents should expose their children to nature from a young age. There is a farm not far from the city to (5) _____ hundreds of families go every weekend. There, city kids (6) _____ might not otherwise have had the chance are able to see, and even to touch, a wide variety of living things. By encountering animals (7) _____ are real, not just pictures, I believe students learn the important lesson (8) _____ these are living creatures worthy of respect and compassion, just like us.

7B As if, as though, as, the way, and *like*

When *as* introduces a clause expressing a comparison, subject-verb inversion can occur in affirmative sentences.

With *do*: Marissa has a lot of trouble accepting change, **as does Trina**.

With auxiliary verbs: Mitt has obtained his painting restoration license, **as has his brother**.

With modals: Grandma would tell us stories of the old days, **as would Grandpa**.

With *be*: Marcel is wary of technology, **as is his whole family**.

When both clauses have the same subject, *as if* and *as though* clauses with adjectives or past participles are frequently shortened by removing the subject and *be*.

The curator held on tightly to the ancient vase with both hands, **as though (she were)** terrified that someone would steal it.

Marvin sat motionless in front of his new media center, **as if (he were)** glued to the chair.

1 Combine these sentences using a clause expressing comparison with *as*. Be sure to use subject-verb inversion.

1. The people of my country welcomed the Internet age. People all over the world welcomed it too.

   The people of my country welcomed the Internet age, as did people all over the world.

2. Ariel will try to block the changes. Martina will try to block them too.

3. Clark is a member of the town's historical society. Taylor is a member as well.

4. Yukio went to a traditional Chinese opera last night. Jin went too.

5. The teacher's union is advocating a four-day workweek. The transit workers' union is advocating this as well.

6. I've given up my car and am taking public transportation now. Several of my co-workers are taking public transportation too.

7. I can cope well with changes. My wife can cope well with changes too.

8. Min Chul believes that it is often foolish to resist change. Cho also believes that it is often foolish to do so.

2 Rewrite the sentences, shortening the longer clauses and lengthening the shorter clauses. Follow the model in the grammar box above.

1. Guests in the theater felt a strange sensation, as if transported back in time.

   Guests in the theater felt a strange sensation, as if they had been transported back in time.

2. That family lives without electricity, as though they were trapped in the 1800s.

3. The music sounded perfectly authentic, as if it were conducted by Beethoven himself.

4. That kid's clothes looked too big for him, as though borrowed from an older brother.

5. My grandmother looks odd in that old photo, as if she were annoyed.

8A Placement of direct and indirect objects

The following verbs are commonly used with both a direct and indirect object.

bring   hand   order   pay   serve
give   make   owe   promise   throw

When the direct object is a pronoun, it goes before the indirect object. When the indirect object is a pronoun, it can go before or after the direct object.
The boss owes **it to Sid**. (*it* = direct object)
The boss owes **him a month's salary**. (*him* = indirect object)
The boss owes **a month's salary to him**. (*him* = indirect object)

When both objects are pronouns, only one pattern is possible: direct object + *to* + indirect object.
The boss owes **it to him**.

1 Complete the sentences using the words in parentheses. Write each sentence in two different ways.

1. Finally, the waiter brought . . . (our dinners / us)

   Finally, the waiter brought us our dinners.

   Finally, the waiter brought our dinners to us.

2. After an hour of searching, the clerk gave . . . (a suitable pair of shoes / me)

3. At that restaurant, they won't serve . . . (your meal / you) unless you pay for it in advance.

4. I didn't have any cash, so I handed . . . (my credit card / the clerk)

5. The potter at that shop promised . . . (a beautiful vase / my mother)

6. I don't have any more cash, but I can pay . . . (the rest / you) tomorrow.

2 Rewrite the following sentences in as many ways as possible using pronouns in place of the nouns in boldface.

1. The clerk gave **Maria the wrong blouse**.

   The clerk gave her the wrong blouse. The clerk gave the wrong blouse to her.
   The clerk gave it to Maria. The clerk gave it to her.

2. The salesman sold **his last vacuum** to **John**.

3. That company still owes **Michael one week's pay**.

4. The real estate agent didn't mention the **leaky roof** to **the customers**.

5. The travel guide found **two wonderful antique shops** for **the tourists**.

6. Marcia reminded Mark that he had promised **a diamond ring** to **her**.

7. The hotel chef made **my mother an omelet**.

8. After the receipt was printed, the clerk handed **Eleanor a pen**.

8B Verbs in the subjunctive

The following verbs can be followed by a *that* clause with a subjunctive verb.

advise   beg   ensure   require
ask   concede   prefer   stipulate

He **advised that** his students **be** on time.

The negative subjunctive is formed with *not* and the base form of the verb.
The advertising executive's contract required that he **not receive** a bonus that year.

The passive form of the subjunctive is formed by *be* + past participle.
The sponsors asked that their product **be featured** prominently in the movie.
The manufacturers preferred that their shaving cream **not be endorsed** by misbehaving stars.

1 Complete the sentences using the subjunctive form of the verbs in the box. Verbs may be used more than once.

broadcast	give	remove
contain	prevent	send

1. The store manager conceded that the customer __be given__ a refund.

2. A new law proposes that telemarketers _____ from calling after 8:00 P.M.

3. It is required that an advertisement _____ any false information.

4. The university council advised that the company _____ from advertising on campus.

5. The contract clearly stipulates that the station _____ our ads 24 hours a day.

6. The customer insisted that she _____ a free sample of the perfume.

7. I would prefer that companies _____ me spam e-mail of any kind.

8. We begged that we _____ from the telemarketer's calling list.

2 Complete the sentences using an appropriate form of the verb in parentheses. Use the subjunctive when possible.

1. It's clear that the time devoted to commercials on TV _has increased_ over the past ten years. (increase)

2. She advised that pressure _____ to companies that engage in false advertising. (apply)

3. I learned that my neighbor _____ a guerrilla marketer. (be)

4. The store required that each customer _____ his or her bag for inspection. (open)

5. He stipulated that this advertisement _____ in this month's issue. (place)

6. The actress begged that she _____ in such a cheap commercial. (cast)

7. I discovered that my sister _____ addicted to shopping. (be)

9A Whenever and wherever contrasted with when and where

If *whenever*, *wherever*, *when*, and *where* are followed by subject + *be* + adjective / past participle, the subject and *be* are often deleted. This occurs mainly in formal speech and writing.
Dog owners must take their dogs to the vet **whenever / when** ~~taking them is~~ advisable.
Laws concerning the welfare of helper animals should be enforced **wherever / where** applicable.

Whenever and *wherever* can have the meaning "no matter when / where."
A: My dog doesn't like it when I give her a bath at night.
B: Mine doesn't like it **whenever** I give him a bath!

Whenever and *wherever* can also have the meaning "although I don't know when / where."
We'll have to get together on his birthday, **whenever** that is!
Our dog was found in a park outside of Hicksville, **wherever** that is!

Whenever and *wherever* are rarely used following the focus adverbs *even*, *just*, *right*, and *only*.
My cats show me affection even **when** I'm in a bad mood.

1 Shorten the sentences by crossing out the subject and the form of *be* in the adverbial clause.

1. Dog owners are expected to use leashes to walk their dogs where ~~using those items is~~ required by law.

2. My veterinarian suggested that I buy Barkies brand dog food when Barkies brand is available.

3. Whenever disciplining them is appropriate, owners of intelligent animals must be prepared to discipline their pets.

4. Exotic animals may not be kept as pets wherever keeping such pets is prohibited by law.

5. Whenever it is possible, you should give your horses a chance to run so that their hooves don't become overgrown.

6. Pets need to be given attention every day, not just when giving them attention is convenient.

2 Review the grammar rules on page 71. Complete the sentences using *when*, *whenever*, *where*, or *wherever*.

1. _____When_____ my dog ran out of the yard this morning, I called his name, but he kept on running.

2. _____ somebody walks past my house, my dog growls at him or her.

3. My pet deer can hear me walking even _____ I'm 100 meters away.

4. I'm trying to find an apartment _____ I'll be allowed to have pets.

5. I ordered a parrot through the Internet from a town called Mambucaba, _____ that is!

6. Over the course of the year, _____ I visited her apartment, she seemed to have added another cat. By spring she had 25.

9B Noun clauses with *whoever* and *whatever*

In formal speech and writing, *whoever* is used for the subject and *whomever* is used for the object of a clause. *Whomever* is rare in conversation.

Whoever sees a bird of paradise can't help being impressed by those feathers.

That snake's poison is generally fatal to **whomever** it bites.

When referring to a known and limited group of items, *whichever* can be used to mean "whatever one" or "whatever ones."

There are only two lizards left, an iguana and a chameleon. Take **whichever** you want.

The bear stood its ground against the dogs, ready to strike **whichever** was bold enough to attack.

1 Complete the sentences with *whoever* or *whomever*.

1. My dog isn't much of a guard dog; ____whoever____ gives him a snack becomes his friend forever.

2. The ASPCA reserves the right to deny animal adoption privileges to _____ they choose.

3. The pet store will give the abandoned parrots to _____ they judge able to provide them with a good home.

4. _____ lives in that house should call the exterminator – it's overrun with mice!

5. _____ would get a tiger cub as a pet for his son is incredibly ignorant and irresponsible.

6. Ladies and gentlemen, we apologize for the inconvenience, but we will be administering an avian flu test to _____ we determine to be showing symptoms of the disease.

7. I know my dog looks big and dangerous, but _____ knows him well will tell you that he's as gentle as a lamb.

8. The city dog pound provides free kenneling services to _____ they determine is in financial hardship.

2 Fill in the blanks with *whoever*, *whatever*, or *whichever*.

A woman who lives down the street from me collects animals. She will accept gifts of animals from (1) ____whoever____ gives them to her. And (2) _____ they give to her she accepts, because she is so kind hearted. Last week she received two beautiful kittens, one black and one brown, from a homeless man. She showed them to me, and when I asked if I could have one, she told me to take (3) _____ I wanted. I took the black one, a male. I named him King, and I've had him for a few months now. (4) _____ sees him says he's really adorable. He's also a very intelligent cat; I really think he understands (5) _____ I say to him. I have to admit that I spoil him. He gets (6) _____ he wants for food – chicken, fish, beef – and not cat food from a can. He gets real meat from the supermarket. During the day he sleeps on the sofa or on the easy chair – he generally chooses (7) _____ is sunnier. At night he sleeps up on the bed with me. (8) _____ visits me always says King really lives like a king.

10A   Overview of passives

The passive voice with a modal can be used in short answers.
A: Why wasn't that author awarded the Nobel Prize for literature?
B: I don't know, but he **should have been**. (He should have been awarded the Nobel Prize for literature.)

The verb *get* can also serve as an auxiliary to form the passive voice. It is less formal and primarily used in spoken English. *Get* always indicates a change (with a meaning close to *become*), while *be* can indicate an unchanging state or a dynamic one.
Larry and Natalie **got married** in 2006. (Their wedding occurred in 2006.)
Larry and Natalie **were married** in 2006 when they went to Greece. (Their wedding may have occurred before 2006.)

The verb *get* is also commonly used in expressions such as *get acquainted*, *get arrested*, *get dressed*, *get excited*, *get married*, and *get scared*.

1 Complete the short answers with the appropriate modal in the passive voice.

1. A: Will that Shakespeare class be offered next semester too?
   B: Oh, yes. I'm absolutely sure that it ____will be____ .

2. A: Should text speak be used in essays by some students?
   B: Actually, I think it _____ .

3. A: Could English be overtaken as the main international language someday?
   B: Well, in my opinion it _____ .

4. A: Was the television turned off when we went to bed?
   B: No, it wasn't, but it _____ .

5. A: Would our class have been canceled if the teacher had been sick?
   B: Yes, it _____ . Thank goodness she's not sick!

6. A: Do you think groceries can be safely bought over the Internet?
   B: I'm sure they _____ . I've considered doing it myself.

2 Do you think *be* or *get* is more appropriate in these sentences? Complete them with the correct form of *be* or *get*.

1. While I was reading a book in the bathtub, I heard someone knocking, so I quickly ____got____ dressed and answered the door.

2. The binding _____ already broken when I bought the book, so it must have happened earlier.

3. Sanjay and Afrin had never met, so I gave them a few minutes to _____ acquainted.

4. Martin Luther King, Jr. _____ remembered for his contribution to advancing civil rights for African Americans in the United States.

5. When she saw my father carrying her birthday gift, all of a sudden my little sister _____ really excited and started jumping up and down.

10B Subject-verb agreement with quantifiers

A (*large / small / great*) *number of* always modifies a plural noun. The resulting expression takes a plural verb.
A (*large*) number of students in my English class **were** absent on Friday.

When certain collective nouns, such as *majority* or *minority*, act as a whole unit or a single group, they take a singular verb.
All students can express their opinions, but **the majority rules**.
In the U.S., **Spanish speakers** constitute a linguistic **minority** that **is** growing rapidly.

Majority and *minority* are followed by the plural form of *be* when the complement is a plural noun.
If you ask my father about young people today, he'll tell you that **the majority are slackers**.
Of people who are concerned with using language correctly, only **a small minority are linguists**.

1 Review the rules for quantifiers on page 85. Circle the correct form of the verb. If both forms are possible, circle both.

1. A minority of American English speakers (*understand*)/(*understands*) Australian slang.

2. A great number of my friends *has / have* sharp tongues.

3. You can't trust people with secrets these days. The majority *is / are* gossips.

4. In the parliament, the newly elected majority *is / are* ready to make some changes.

5. A number of hip-hop expressions *has / have* been added to dictionaries.

6. A majority of my friends *has / have* a way with words.

7. There are times when a minority *speak / speaks* louder than a majority.

8. A number of languages *is / are* spoken in India.

2 Complete these sentences with the singular or plural simple present form of the verb in parentheses.

1. Each person _____finds_____ the level of formality he or she is comfortable with. (find)

2. No one _____ the exact number of words in the English language. (know)

3. Most of my friends _____ English fluently. (speak)

4. None of the linking verbs _____ normally used in the passive voice. (be)

5. A lot of people _____ abroad to practice their English. (go)

6. A recent report indicated that one-third of American high school students _____ . (not, graduate)

7. Plenty of my friends _____ to send each other text messages. (like)

8. Every language _____ formal and less formal registers. (have)

9. Every one of my in-laws _____ my ear off on the phone. (talk)

10. All fluent speakers _____ to have an understanding of idiomatic language. (need)

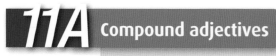

11A Compound adjectives

The following compound adjectives are found written as one word in many dictionaries.

airborne	barefooted	hardheaded	painstaking
airsick	daylong	lightweight	seaworthy
awestruck	downhearted	newfound	

In the comparative form of compound adjectives, *more* and *less* are not followed by hyphens.

a more forward-looking plan   a less easygoing person   a more highly trained applicant

1   Use one-word adjectives from the grammar box above to rewrite the sentences.

1. The flight attendant helped the passengers who felt sick on the airplane.

   The flight attendant helped the airsick passengers.

2. We attended a meeting that lasted from 9:00 in the morning to 6:00 in the evening.

3. The passengers boarded the sturdy vessel that was worthy of making an ocean voyage.

4. The sailors stopped at an island that had only recently been discovered.

5. The star was overwhelmed by the fans who showed their admiration and respect for her.

6. Jason caught a virus that was carried through the air.

2   Combine the words from both boxes to create eight compound adjectives. Check your CD-ROM dictionary for meaning and for hyphen use. Then use the adjectives to complete the sentences.

easy	spell	bound	hearted
forward	tender	fisted	looking
long	tight	going	respected
red	widely	headed	winded

1. In the acting business, blond and brown-haired actors are much more common than _redheaded_ ones.

2. Because of his great experience in international affairs, the president is _____ in political circles.

3. The audience understood that they wouldn't be able to leave for a while; the speaker had a reputation for being _____ .

4. I hope you brought some money; the boss is too _____ to pay.

5. The amazing stunts of the circus performers kept the children _____ .

6. Our country needs a _____ leader, one who can prepare us for crises before they occur.

7. The _____ celebrity could never pass homeless people without giving them some money.

8. I think you should stop worrying about everything and learn to be more _____ .

The following adjectives and adverbs have irregular comparative and superlative forms. They are frequently used in comparative and superlative compound adjectives.

Adjective	Comparative	Superlative	Adverb	Comparative	Superlative
good	better	best	well	better	best
bad	worse	worst	badly	worse	worst
far	farther / further	farthest / furthest	little	less (lesser)	least
			much	more	most
			far	farther / further	farthest / furthest

As with other superlative adjectives, the article *the* is not used when the noun is preceded by a possessive.
Venezuela's **best-known** poet will be reading one of his works at the public library this week.

1 Write sentences as in the example using the information and the superlative form of the comparative adjective.

1. Charlize Theron is / good-looking actress / I ever see
   Charlize Theron is the best-looking actress I've ever seen.

2. My company president is / well-dressed executive / I ever work for

3. That science-fiction story has / far-fetched plot / I ever read

4. Our chief of police is / little-appreciated public servant / our town ever have

5. Mr. Fredericks is / well-loved teacher / our class ever have

6. That player is / bad-tempered guy / our basketball team ever hire

7. Professor Kwan is / much-honored academic / our college ever invite to speak

8. That movie was filmed at / far-flung location / the studio ever use

2 Write sentences using the superlative form of the compound adjective. Be careful to use hyphens and *the* correctly.

1. That company's (lightweight) camera is the Photoflash X25.
   That company's most lightweight camera is the Photoflash X25.
   That company's lightest-weight camera is the Photoflash X25.

2. My uncle's face was (awestruck) in the photograph on the right.

3. Henry was (broad-minded) when it came to questions of cultural difference.

4. I take after my father, who is (hardheaded) man I know.

5. My mother is quite smart, but she's not (well-read) person in the world.

6. To me, Japan's (awe-inspiring) sight is probably Mount Fuji.

7. Perhaps (widely recognized) actress from Malaysia is Michelle Yao.

8. The (low-lying) country in Europe is Holland.

When present or future real conditionals are expressed with *should* at the beginning of the sentence, the base form of the verb is used.
If my brother **decides** to start a business, he'll come to you for financing.
Should my brother **decide** to start a business, he'll come to you for financing.

If you**'re** looking for a competent employee, Ted is your man.
Should you **be** looking for a competent employee, Ted is your man.

Subject-verb inversion in conditional sentences occurs very rarely with *might* and *could*, usually in literary or archaic contexts with adverbs such as *but* or *just*.
Could he **but** win her love, the world would be his.
Might I **just** see my country once more, my heart would find peace.

Other verbs and auxiliaries do not allow subject-verb inversion. Use an *if* clause instead.
If I **can** make the sale, I certainly will.
If they **have** gone out of business, we'll have to find another supplier.
If I **may** speak frankly, I think you're just not doing a good enough job.

1 Rewrite these sentences using *should* at the beginning of the sentence and the base form of the verb.

1. If Sven goes into business for himself, I'm sure he'll do very well.

   Should Sven go into business for himself, I'm sure he'll do very well.

2. If Annie gets a raise, she'll be able to pay her college debts.

3. If Shin is sick tomorrow, would you be able to work in place of him?

4. If you find yourself swamped by work, hire yourself an assistant.

5. If a business is set up in a good location, customers will naturally come.

6. If a problem arises, you need to find a way to work around it.

7. If there's a chance of failure, I'd rather not take the risk.

8. If there's a lot of demand for a product, the price naturally rises.

2 Review the grammar rules on page 97. Check (✓) the sentences that can be inverted. Then rewrite them using subject-verb inversion.

☑ 1. If you asked him, he'd tell you the secret of his success.

   Were you to ask him, he'd tell you the secret of his success.

☐ 2. If I have some extra money at the end of the year, I'll invest it.

☐ 3. If his boss hadn't been working against him, Jake would have been promoted.

☐ 4. If I may suggest, I think you should ask for a promotion.

☐ 5. If I could just win the gold medal, I'd be happier than the richest man.

☐ 6. If I hadn't finished my business degree, I'd have a much lower salary.

☐ 7. If they were aware of the risk, they would quickly patent their idea.

☐ 8. If Tamara hadn't spoken out, the boss would have ignored her.

☐ 9. If we can have a meeting, we could perhaps find a better solution.

☐ 10. If Anita hadn't taken risks, she would never have become successful.

12B Adverb clauses of condition

In the event (*that*) and (*just*) *in case* also introduce a condition on which another situation depends. *In the event* (*that*) is more formal.
In the event that a replacement cannot be found, you'll have to take on extra responsibilities.
Here's a number to call **just in case** the copy machine breaks down.

Whether or not is used instead of *if* to introduce a condition on which another situation depends. *Or not* is placed directly after *whether* or at the end of the clause.
Whether or not it involves travel, I'm going to have to take this job.
Whether it involves travel **or not**, I'm going to have to take this job.

Even if introduces a condition which, if it is true, doesn't affect the outcome of a situation. It is frequently used with *still*.
I'm (**still**) going to call in sick tomorrow **even if** I'm not actually sick.

If only introduces a condition that the speaker strongly wishes to be true.
If only I had known about that job opening, I would have applied for it immediately.

1 Match the clauses to make logical conditional sentences.

1. If only I hadn't insulted my boss, _e_
2. Whether you feel happy inside or not, ____
3. Even if you have great leadership skills, ____
4. Just in case you didn't get the memo, ____
5. If only I could wear casual clothes to work, ____
6. Whether or not the schedule is flexible, ____
7. Even if my company offers me a raise, ____
8. In case I get permanently disabled, ____

a. here's a copy for your files.
b. I wouldn't have to spend so much money on suits.
c. I'll collect half my current salary for five years.
d. I'm still going to take a job with another firm.
e. I'm sure he wouldn't have fired me.
f. the manager wants you to smile for the customers.
g. you can't be forced to work more than 40 hours a week.
h. you still have to earn the workers' respect.

2 Circle the choice that best completes the sentence.

1. (*Just in case*)/ *If only* I have to go on a business trip this week, I've kept my schedule open.
2. *Even if / Assuming that* the weather is nice, this weekend's company picnic should be fun.
3. *In the event that / Whether or not* I receive training, I'm still not confident in my abilities.
4. *Even if / If only* I were in charge of hiring people, I'd give everybody a pay raise.
5. *Provided that / Just in case* employees do what is required, salaries are increased every year.

Units 1-12 Self-study

Unit 1 Self-study

1. Reunion

listening

A 🔘 **Track 1** Listen to Chris making announcements. What is the occasion? Check (✓) the correct answer.

☐ a. the first class reunion after five years

✓ ☐ b. the first class reunion after ten years

NO ☒ c. the second class reunion after ten years

B 🔘 Listen again. Number these events from 1 to 5 in the order the announcer says they will happen.

3 __ a. ballgame 10 am.

2 __ b. band playing

1 __ c. prize announcements

5 __ d. buffet

4 __ e. barbeque 12 pm.

C 🔘 Look at this excerpt from the announcements. How does Chris feel about the photos he's in? Check (✓) the correct answer. Then listen again and check.

Chris: I have to say that there are some of me that have resurfaced which I'd hoped never to see again. I've had to relive some very painful memories and some very bad haircuts . . .

☒ a. He thinks they're embarrassing but funny.

☐ b. He's annoyed with the people who sent them in.

☐ c. He's upset by seeing them again.

2. Phrasal verbs

vocabulary

CD-ROM Look at the audio script of the reunion announcements on page 142. Use your CD-ROM dictionary to find the phrasal verbs in boldface that have these definitions.

1. to appear or come to your attention _____

2. to make something very quickly _____

3. to search for someone or something _____

4. to stop working or not be successful _____

5. to prepare or arrange something for use _____

6. to look at, examine, think of, or deal with a set of things _____

7. to arrive for a gathering or event _____

Unit 2 Self-study

1. Dress for success

listening

A Track 2 Listen to a radio show about preparing for a job interview. What does the guest speaker feel is the most important thing about appearance at job interviews? Check (✓) the correct answer.

- ☒ a. fashionable clothes
- ☒ b. looking like everyone else
- ☐ c. good grooming

B Listen again. Does the image consultant encourage (*E*) or discourage (*D*) these things? Or does he not say (*N*)? Write the correct letter.

- _N_ 1. a conservative suit
- _E_ 2. polished shoes
- _N_ 3. clean teeth
- _N_ 4. conservative shoes
- _N_ 5. bold jewelry that makes a statement
- _E_ 6. a lot of cologne or aftershave
- _D_ 7. fashionable clothes
- _D_ 8. extreme styles

C Look at this excerpt from the show. Why does the host ask this question? Check (✓) the correct answer. Then listen again and check.

Host: Is it fair that people are judged by how they look?

Andy: No, probably not. But that is what happens.

- ☐ a. He is expressing an opinion.
- ☐ b. He is asking for information.
- ☐ c. He is asking for Andy's opinion.

2. Parts of speech

vocabulary

A CD-ROM Look at this excerpt from the radio show. Use your CD-ROM dictionary to help you answer the questions.

Andy: Dress so that you look as though you fit in with the new environment. Do a little research.

1. What part of speech is *research* in this context? _____
2. How many parts of speech can *research* be? _____
3. Does the word stress change for each part of speech? _____

B CD-ROM Check (✓) the correct parts of speech. Use your CD-ROM dictionary.

	Noun	Verb	Adjective
1. dress	✓	✓	✓
2. look			
3. rule			
4. subtle			
5. style			

Unit 3 Self-study

1. Constantly connected

listening

A 🔘 **Track 3** Listen to a radio show called *Let's Lighten Up a Little*. What is the main focus of the show this week?

- ☐ a. the stress of being "connected" or "contactable" all the time
- ☐ b. time management
- ☐ c. information overload

B 🔘 Listen again. Are these statements true or false? Check (✓) the correct answer.

	True	False
1. Kyoko is a psychiatrist.	☐	☐
2. Psychiatrists are affected by information overload.	☐	☐
3. Kyoko feels that it is easy to keep up with all the new medical information.	☐	☐
4. Kyoko thinks that shopping online is a waste of time.	☐	☐
5. Brains need to relax.	☐	☐

C 🔘 Look at this excerpt from the show. How much is Kyoko affected by information overload? Check (✓) the correct answer. Then listen again and check.

Adam: Are you yourself affected by it?

Kyoko: Oh, yes.

- ☐ a. not very affected
- ☐ b. somewhat affected
- ☐ c. very affected

2. Prepositions

vocabulary

A Look at the audio script of the radio show on page 143. What are the missing prepositions in the excerpt?

Well, Adam, it's the feeling of not being able to keep up (1) _____ all the information that's available (2) _____ us – and not having the time or the skill to keep it (3) _____ control, keep it organized.

B CD-ROM Use your CD-ROM dictionary to find out which prepositions follow these verbs and adjectives. Some prepositions are used more than once.

by	for	in	of	on	with

1. aware _____
2. happy _____
3. proud _____
4. typical _____
5. apologize _____
6. surprised _____
7. concentrate _____
8. interested _____

Unit 4 Self-study

1. Robert Ripley

listening

A **Track 4** Listen to a discussion about Robert Ripley. What was he best known for?

- ☐ a. being a professional athlete
- ☐ b. being a cartoonist
- ☐ c. being a boat collector

B Listen again. Check (✓) the facts you hear about Robert Ripley.

- ☐ a. He collected cars.
- ☐ b. He was a good driver.
- ☐ c. He collected Chinese art.
- ☐ d. He dressed conservatively.
- ☐ e. He was a radio broadcaster, then had a TV show.

C Look at this excerpt from the discussion. Why does Nick say this? Check (✓) the correct answer. Then listen again and check.

Nick: So tell us, Sam, what's so special about Robert Ripley? I've heard a lot of, well, *different* opinions about the man.

- ☐ a. He has heard some positive things about Ripley.
- ☐ b. He has heard some negative things about Ripley.
- ☐ c. He doesn't know anything about Ripley.

2. Adjectives: Opposites

vocabulary

A **CD-ROM** Look at the audio script of the show on page 143. Use your CD-ROM dictionary to match each adjective in boldface with its definition.

1. strange or unusual, sometimes in an amusing way ____   a. eccentric
2. done as a job, or relating to a skilled type of work ____   b. outrageous
3. unusual and surprising ____   c. remarkable
4. unacceptable, shocking, possibly offensive ____   d. professional

B **CD-ROM** Use your CD-ROM dictionary to match the adjectives on the left with their synonyms on the right. (Tip: use the thesaurus)

1. dependable ____   a. genuine
2. gullible ____   b. vengeful
3. indecisive ____   c. wishy-washy
4. methodical ____   d. foolish
5. sincere ____   e. meticulous
6. vindictive ____   f. reliable

Unit 5 Self-study

1. Nature's soap opera

listening

A 🔘 **Track 5** Listen to an interview with a TV documentary filmmaker. What types of programs does he make?

☐ a. political science programs

☐ b. reality, hidden-camera comedy programs

☐ c. science and nature programs

B 🔘 Listen again. Are these statements true or false? Check (✓) the correct answer.

	True	False
1. *River Watch* is on every night.	☐	☐
2. There is quite a lot of time spent on editing.	☐	☐
3. There are 60 cameras used to film the program.	☐	☐
4. The bald eagle nest on *River Watch* is the largest ever recorded.	☐	☐
5. The bald eagle story is the only one featured on *River Watch*.	☐	☐

C 🔘 Look at this excerpt from the interview. What do you think Dave means? Check (✓) the correct answer. Then listen again and check.

Mandy: Does the crew get as involved as the viewers, or have you seen so much of it that it's lost some of its power?

Dave: Oh, no. No. Not at all.

☐ a. He and the crew aren't affected emotionally by the animals they film.

☐ b. They are very affected by the animals they film.

☐ c. They are somewhat affected by the animals they film.

2. Adverbs and word stress

vocabulary

A CD-ROM Look at these definitions for some of the adverbs used in the interview. Use your CD-ROM dictionary to match each adverb with its definition.

1. completely; beyond any doubt ____   a. absolutely

2. easily seen ____   b. actually

3. likely, although not certain ____   c. obviously

4. unexpectedly ____   d. presumably

5. used to say something true ____   e. surprisingly

B CD-ROM Use your CD-ROM dictionary to mark the stress on these words. Underline the stressed syllable.

1. surprisingly   3. obviously   5. instinctively

2. unquestionably   4. presumably   6. actually

Unit 6 Self-study

1. Music man

listening

A 🔘 **Track 6** Listen to a lecture about Alan Lomax. What type of music was he most interested in?

- ☐ a. classical
- ☐ b. hip-hop and reggae
- ☐ c. folk and blues

B 🔘 Listen again. Put these events in the correct order.

- ____ a. Lomax recorded Lead Belly in prison.
- ____ b. Lomax traveled with his father to compile a book of folk songs.
- ____ c. Lomax traveled to other countries to record music.
- ____ d. Lomax began helping his father gather his songs.
- ____ e. Lead Belly songs were covered by other musicians.

C 🔘 Look at this excerpt from the talk. What does the professor mean? Check (✓) the correct answer. Then listen again and check.

Professor: It might be a little easier to ask which instruments he *didn't* play.

- ☐ a. Lead Belly was a songwriter, not a performer.
- ☐ b. Lead Belly didn't really play many instruments.
- ☐ c. Lead Belly played a lot of instruments.

2. Word building

vocabulary

A **CD-ROM** In the listening, the professor mentions "musicology." The suffix *-ology* was added to *music* to make a noun. What subject do each of these terms refer to?

1. anthropology _____
2. biology _____
3. cardiology _____
4. geology _____
5. ornithology _____
6. etymology _____

B **CD-ROM** Use your CD-ROM dictionary to complete this table.

Noun	Person noun	Verb	Adjective	Adverb
1. achievement	achiever			—
2. collection				—
3.	—			commercially
4.	musician	—	musical	
5.		perform	—	—

Unit 7 Self-study

1. Farmers' markets

listening

A **Track 7** Listen to a conversation between two friends, Emma and Lucy. What does Emma think is surprising about the farmers' market?

☐ a. The food is fresher.

☐ b. There is a dairy stall.

☐ c. The food is generally cheaper.

B Listen again. Check the items that are mentioned.

☐ a. apricots   ☐ g. strawberries

☐ b. candles   ☐ h. onions

☐ c. cheese   ☐ i. potatoes

☐ d. chocolate   ☐ j. plants

☐ e. coffee   ☐ k. natural cosmetics

☐ f. yogurt   ☐ l. homemade bread

C Look at this excerpt from the conversation. Check (✓) the correct interpretation of the sentence. Then listen again and check.

Lucy: For instance, the strawberries at the supermarket, which were flown in and not especially fresh, were about a dollar a pound more.

☐ a. Some of the strawberries at the supermarket were flown in and not very fresh.

☐ b. All of the strawberries at the supermarket were flown in and not very fresh.

2. Comparatives

vocabulary

A **CD-ROM** Look at the audio script of the conversation on page 145. Use your CD-ROM dictionary to find the comparatives in boldface that have these definitions.

a. healthier   _____

b. more morally acceptable   _____

c. more worried about _____

B **CD-ROM** Use your CD-ROM dictionary to check which words can be a noun, a verb, or both. Underline which syllable is stressed in each form.

	Noun	Verb
1. contract		
2. produce		
3. record		
4. release		
5. wonder		

Unit 8 Self-study

1. Shopping styles

listening

A **Track 8** Listen to a conversation between Andrea and Pauline. Why didn't Pauline buy the coat? Check (✓) the correct answer.

☐ a. The salesperson was at lunch.

☐ b. She didn't really like the coat.

☐ c. The salesperson was too forceful.

B Listen again. Are these statements true or false? Check (✓) the correct answer.

	True	False
1. Andrea appreciates being left alone by salespeople.	☐	☐
2. Pauline thinks salespeople should suggest items to customers.	☐	☐
3. Pauline generally agrees with her husband's shopping decisions.	☐	☐
4. Andrea thinks the things her sister suggests she buy are bargains.	☐	☐
5. Pauline thought some of the customers at Williams' were unreasonable.	☐	☐

C Look at this excerpt from the conversation. Who is Andrea laughing at? Check (✓) the correct answer. Then listen again and check.

Andrea: I buy it. Then, after she leaves, I take it back and donate it *back* to the thrift shop.

☐ a. herself

☐ b. the thrift shop salesperson

☐ c. her friend

2. Double meanings

vocabulary

A CD-ROM Look at the audio script of the conversation on page 145. Use your CD-ROM dictionary to find the words in boldface that have these definitions.

1. a group or collection of twelve _____

2. an unlucky or disappointing situation _____

3. extremely unpleasant _____

4. something sold for a price that is lower than usual or lower than its value _____

5. to give something without wanting anything in exchange _____

6. trying too hard to persuade someone to do something _____

B CD-ROM Which of these words have more than one meaning? Use your CD-ROM dictionary. Check (✓) the words that have more than one meaning.

☐ 1. alone   ☐ 3. bunch   ☐ 5. stuff   ☐ 7. leaves

☐ 2. item   ☐ 4. cart   ☐ 6. fortune   ☐ 8. pair

Unit 9 Self-study

1. Animal behaviorists

listening

A 🔘 **Track 9** Listen to an interview about working with animals. What are the two levels of certification for animal behaviorists?

1. _____ Applied Animal Behaviorist

2. _____ Applied Animal Behaviorist

B 🔘 Listen again. Answer the questions.

1. Which types of animals does Fay mention? Check (✓) the types of animals you hear.

☐ a. aquarium fish   ☐ d. farm animals

☐ b. pets   ☐ e. zoo animals

☐ c. insects   ☐ f. wild animals

2. Which professions do animal behaviorists come from? Check (✓) the professions she lists.

☐ a. agriculture   ☐ e. ecology

☐ b. animal science   ☐ f. environmental science

☐ c. biology   ☐ g. psychology

☐ d. botany   ☐ h. zoology

C 🔘 Look at this excerpt from the interview. How does Fay feel when she says the sentence below? Check (✓) the correct answer. Then listen again and check.

Fay: Yes, you could put it that way.

☐ a. She's glad that Phil understands.

☐ b. She's annoyed because Phil doesn't seem to take the profession seriously.

☐ c. She's annoyed because Phil doesn't like animals.

2. Animal vocabulary

vocabulary

CD-ROM In the interview, Fay refers to a group of cows as a *herd*. Use your CD-ROM dictionary to put the animals in the box under the correct collective noun.

birds   cows   elephants   fish   goats   sheep

Flock	Herd	School
	cows	

Unit 10 Self-study

1. English as a Lingua Franca

listening

A **Track 10** Listen to a lecture about English as a Lingua Franca. Which of these descriptions best defines English as a Lingua Franca? Check (✓) the correct answer.

☐ a. a standard variety of English

☐ b. a mixture of American and British Standard English

☐ c. an evolving variety or varieties of English

B Listen again. Are these statements true or false? Check (✓) the correct answer.

	True	False
1. The majority of academic articles are in English.	☐	☐
2. More than two billion people speak English.	☐	☐
3. Most English speakers are native speakers.	☐	☐
4. Modern English grammar prescribes how English should be used.	☐	☐

C Look at this excerpt from the lecture. Why does the professor hesitate after the student gives a definition of *ELF*? Check (✓) the correct answer. Then listen again and check.

Clea: It's basically a common language used between groups that speak different languages to conduct business, commerce, isn't it?

Professor: Well, yes, business, commerce – life.

☐ a. The professor thinks the definition is too narrow.

☐ b. The professor can't understand what she means.

☐ c. The professor thinks the definition is too general.

2. Guidewords

vocabulary

A **CD-ROM** In the listening, the professor says people are "calling for" a new kind of dictionary. Which of these guidewords best matches what the professor means by "call"?

a. name   c. say   e. consider   g. suggest strongly
b. telephone   d. ask to come f. come to get

B **CD-ROM** Now match these example sentences with the correct guideword from the box above. Use your CD-ROM dictionary to check your answers.

1. I'll **call** for you around noon. Be ready! ____

2. I **called** last night and left a message. ____

3. I wouldn't **call** him a friend – he's just someone I met. ____

4. "Answer 'Here!' when I **call** your name," the teacher said. ____

Unit 11 Self-study

1. Life coaching

listening

A 🔘 **Track 11** Listen to a program about life coaching. What does Yolanda say the key difference is between life coaching and counseling?

☐ a. Counseling is more action-oriented.

☐ b. Life coaching is more directive.

☐ c. She doesn't think there is a difference; it's just a new term.

B 🔘 Listen again. What benefits of life coaching does Yolanda mention? Check (✓) the benefits you hear.

☐ a. Life coaches believe in you.

☐ b. Life coaches can help you set goals.

☐ c. Life coaches can help you improve your sports technique.

☐ d. Life coaches can help set self-imposed limitations.

☐ e. Life coaches can help break or change deeply engrained goals.

C 🔘 Look at this excerpt from the program. How does May feel about life coaching? Check (✓) the correct answer. Then listen again and check.

May: Now, isn't life coaching really just a newly invented name for counseling or therapy?

☐ a. She's skeptical of its value.

☐ b. She's convinced of its value.

☐ c. She thinks life coaching and counseling or therapy are the same.

2. Formal and informal language

vocabulary

A **CD-ROM** In the listening, Yolanda says, "And, on the surface, that may appear to be so." Which definition for *appear* is she using? Check (✓) the correct answer.

☐ a. to become noticeable or to be present

☐ b. to be made available

☐ c. to seem

B **CD-ROM** Use your CD-ROM dictionary to match the informal words with their formal equivalents below. (Tip: Use the thesaurus)

a. need	d. seem	g. stop
b. get	e. shorten	h. tell
c. keep	f. show	i. use

1. appear _d_   4. decrease ___   7. obtain ___

2. cease ___   5. demonstrate ___   8. require ___

3. consume ___   6. inform ___   9. retain ___

Unit 12 Self-study

1 Time out

listening **A** 🔘 **Track 12** Listen to a conversation between two friends. What is the main topic of their conversation? Check (✓) the correct answer.

☐ a. what they did over the holidays

☐ b. taking a year off

☐ c. the Internet

B 🔘 Listen again. Are these statements true or false? Check (✓) the correct answer.

	True	False
1. Matt's father is glad that he didn't go to Africa.	☐	☐
2. Matt's father is a doctor.	☐	☐
3. Both Matt and Harry are interested in wildlife conservation.	☐	☐
4. Both Matt and Harry are only interested in projects that pay well.	☐	☐
5. They both agree that it is important to choose projects in your area.	☐	☐

C 🔘 Look at this excerpt from the conversation. Why does Harry say this? Check (✓) the correct answer. Then listen again and check.

Harry: Career Man is thinking about taking a year off?

☐ a. He thinks it's a bad idea.

☐ b. He admires Matt's interest in having a career.

☐ c. He thinks it's a surprising choice for Matt.

2 Phrasal verbs

vocabulary **A** CD-ROM Look at the phrasal verbs in boldface in the audio script of the conversation on page 147. Use your CD-ROM dictionary to match each phrasal verb with its correct definition.

1. bring on (something) ____   a. to cause something to happen

2. get (something) out of (something) ____   b. to happen or develop in a particular way

3. look into ____   c. to obtain something by doing something

4 work out ____   d. to try to find out about something

B CD-ROM Complete the sentences with the phrasal verbs from Exercise A. Use your CD-ROM dictionary to help.

1. I actually _____ a lot _____ the lecture. I'm glad I went.

2. I think the loud music _____ my headache _____ .

3. If you're interested in going, I'll _____ _____ making a reservation.

4. We wanted to go to the restaurant, but it didn't _____ _____ .

Self-study audio scripts

Unit 1 Self-study

Chris: Hello everybody, and welcome to the reunion. It's hard to believe, seeing you all together again, that our college graduation was ten years ago. I just want to **run through** a few announcements and announce a few prizes.

First, the buffet will open at 8:30. We are very lucky to have some great cooks among our former classmates who have **whipped** all this **up**.

We'll have a slide show during dinner. Thanks for all the photos you sent in. I have to say that there are some of me that have resurfaced which I'd hoped never to see again. I've had to relive some very painful memories and some very bad haircuts, thanks to them. On the other hand, it's nice to be reminded that I used to have hair to cut.

The band, Random Acts of Kindness, whom you may recall from their younger days, have reunited for one night only. They'll be setting up soon and will start playing at 9:00. Sorry, what's that? Oh, right. Apparently Seth hasn't **shown up** yet. His car **broke down**? Some things never change. Um, but we are sure he will **turn up** eventually, right? OK.

We've got some excellent door prizes, which we'll be announcing in just a few minutes. Then tomorrow, we have the picnic and ballgame. That will be in the park. I think the ballgame is due to start at ten in the morning. Seth's one of the captains? Better make that 10:30, then. You'll probably have worked up a pretty good appetite after the game, so we'll move on to the picnic after. And I think there's going to be a barbeque there, is that right?

Audience: Yeah – we'll probably start cooking around 12:00.

Chris: Excellent.

Now, just before we announce those prizes, I'd like to say a big thank you to Karla Romero for organizing all this. She is the one who **set up** the website and then **tracked** everyone **down**, from some very far-flung places. So, thank you very much, Karla.

OK, door prizes! Jenny, are you and the door prize team . . .

Unit 2 Self-study

Host: Hello, and welcome back to *Job Search*. Today we're lucky to have Andy Watkins from *Image* magazine here to talk to us about dressing for success at job interviews. Welcome to the show, Andy.

Andy: Thanks, Josh. It's good to be here.

Host: Now, Andy, you're a trained and experienced image consultant. Tell us, how important is it to think about what to wear at a job interview?

Andy: Well, it's crucial. Most of the first impressions we make are visual – based on how we look, rather than what we say. And that happens in the first 30 seconds. As they say, you only get one chance to make a good first impression.

Host: Right. So what do you advise people to wear?

Andy: Dress so that you look as though you fit in with the new environment. Do a little research. Find out what people tend to wear to work. Stop by to pick up some information about the company – and look at how people are dressed.

As a rule, though, it's better to be too formal rather than too casual. A conservative, stylish suit is a good look for both men and women.

But it's not just wearing the right clothes. What is absolutely essential is good grooming. The best looking suit in the world won't make up for sloppy grooming. Polished shoes, a good haircut, clean fingernails, and minimal jewelry are key details. We also discourage job seekers from wearing a lot of cologne or aftershave.

Host: What about fashionable clothes? Do you advise people against wearing trendy outfits?

Andy: No, not necessarily. It's OK to be stylish, but be subtle. You are making a statement about yourself. Make sure you know what you are saying.

Host: Is it fair that people are judged by how they look?

Andy: No, probably not. But that is what happens. What employers do is take shortcuts to save time. What strikes employers in interviews is how you look. It's an easy shortcut.

Host: We've got a caller on the line. Clare, what question do you have for Andy?

Clare: Hi. Well, I wondered what Andy thinks about giving a false first impression. I mean, my style is pretty quirky. When I'm choosing what to wear for an interview, I sort of think that I should wear what I normally wear.

Andy: I'd encourage you to tone down extreme styles for an interview. For example . . .

Unit 3 Self-study

Adam: Hello out there! It's time for another installment of *Let's Lighten Up a Little*, the show that tries to make living in the high-tech world a little less stressful.

Last week we looked at the modern-day phenomenon of being connected or contactable all the time – a situation many of us are becoming increasingly fed up with.

This week we'll be looking at dealing with information overload. And we've got psychiatrist Kyoko Norida here to talk to us today. Welcome, Kyoko.

Kyoko: Thanks very much, Adam.

Adam: So, Kyoko, can you start by defining *information overload* for us?

Kyoko: Well, Adam, it's the feeling of not being able to keep up with all the information that's available to us – and not having the time or the skill to keep it under control, keep it organized.

Adam: Are you yourself affected by it?

Kyoko: Oh, yes. Being a psychiatrist, I try to keep up with the vast amount of medical knowledge that is constantly emerging. It's just not realistic. In fact, it's impossible, and it has been for a long time.

Adam: Right. So what can we do?

Kyoko: Well, I've got two suggestions. First, reduce your information intake.

Adam: Wait a minute. You're suggesting that we cut down on the amount of information we take in – even though we feel like we're not taking in enough?

Kyoko: That's right. The truth is that you probably don't need a lot of the information you're consuming. That's because a lot of what you're taking in is random.

That leads me to the second point: Set time limits and consume information more systematically. If you see something that looks interesting, bookmark it. Come back to it later, during your play time.

This will help you organize your information and your time. When you are working, work. Then, having finished the work you need to do, go on the Internet to shop for a birthday present or play a game or whatever.

The other benefit is that, by limiting the amount of time we allow our brains to take in information, we give them some time to relax. Being constantly on call, our brains get tired and don't function as well as they should.

You'll find that both your work and your play time are more effective.

Adam: Well, that sounds like good advice. I'm going to try to break a few bad habits. Kyoko's new book . . .

Unit 4 Self-study

Nick: Hello, and welcome to *Profiles*. On the show tonight we have the well-known cartoonist Sam Harris talking about one of *his* heroes – Robert Ripley.

So tell us, Sam, what's so special about Robert Ripley? I've heard a lot of, well, *different* opinions about the man.

Sam: Well, Nick, there are people who claim that he lied about certain events in his life, but even those people can't deny that he was an amazing cartoonist, a great traveler, and extremely **eccentric**.

Nick: I see. So why do you call him eccentric?

Sam: Well, how else would you describe someone who has an extensive collection of cars – but never learned to drive? But that's not all.

We're talking about a man who spent his life tracking down the strangest and most unusual things he could find. It is believed that he visited 198 countries in his lifetime – and remember, that was in the early 1900s.

He was fascinated by Chinese culture and even bought a real Chinese junk, a huge sailboat, to add to his collection of boats.

But some people feel that *he* was the strangest thing in his collection. He dressed in **outrageous**, brightly colored clothes. His appearance was described by one of his friends as "a paint factory that got hit by lightning."

Nick: So tell us about his career as a cartoonist.

Sam: He didn't start out as a cartoonist, actually. He wanted to be a **professional** baseball player – and he was. But he injured his arm in his first professional ballgame and never played again.

So that's when he became a professional artist. His first job was as a sports cartoonist. One day he was having problems finding enough for his column, so he drew pictures of some unusual sports events – a backward race and a long jump on ice – and the strange and unusual became his specialty. His column was renamed "Believe It or Not!"

Nick: So, it was a lucky accident?

Sam: That's right.

Nick: Incredible! Well, Ripley went on to become first a radio broadcaster, then had a television show, didn't he?

Sam: Uh huh. He was a **remarkable** man. Sadly, he completed only 13 episodes . . .

Unit 5 Self-study

Mandy: Good afternoon. I'm Mandy Cole, and welcome to *Outside Story*. On the show today, we'll be talking to Dr. Dave Greenaway, the man behind the camera in some of your favorite TV shows.

Now, Dave, you've got what is unquestionably the top nature show on TV at the moment – *River Watch*. Can you tell us a bit about it? What have some of the challenges been?

Dave: Well, Mandy, obviously, one of the biggest challenges with *River Watch* is the fact that it's on every night of the week. The episodes are so close together, and we have so many cameras constantly filming the river that we don't have time to do much editing.

Mandy: I suppose that you have so much action on film that it's hard to choose what to use. Is that the case?

Dave: Well, actually, yes. We do have days when we've got too much action, but it's not always the action we want.

One of the biggest factors in choosing material is probably the minidramas or the animals themselves. The day-to-day soap operas on the river are absolutely fascinating. Not surprisingly, our viewers want to know what happens next – and basically, nature is unpredictable. Fortunately, we've got 60 cameras along and under the river.

Mandy: Of all the stories on *River Watch*, it's the bald eagle nest saga that has definitely got me hooked. They really are incredible birds. How big is that nest?

Dave: It's five feet wide, ten feet deep and probably weighs about a ton. But that's not the biggest on record – that one was a whopping ten feet wide, 20 feet deep and weighed in at two tons.

Mandy: The footage last month when one of the chicks left the nest, but wasn't strong enough to fly – it was so gripping. Does the crew get as involved as the viewers, or have you seen so much of it that it's lost some of its power?

Dave: Oh, no. No. Not at all. We get just as caught up in it as the viewers, more so, actually. We were all very relieved when the adults continued to feed the chick on the ground. The first successful flight brought tears to everybody's eyes. It was so moving.

Mandy: Presumably one of the other big attractions is white-tailed deer . . .

Unit 6 Self-study

Professor: Good morning everybody. We've got a lot to get through today, so I'd like to get started right away, if you don't mind.

I hope you've downloaded the notes for today's talk – it's Musicology 101 – Alan Lomax. Can I just see a show of hands? Great.

OK, so Alan Lomax has been described as one of the most important figures in the preservation of American folk music. He also pioneered the study of world music.

Yes, Sylvia, you have a question?

Sylvia: Can you give us some background on how Alan Lomax got his start in music?

Professor: Sure, Sylvia. Well, from childhood, Lomax would help his father, John, in his song-gathering. At that time, John Lomax was the country's preeminent collector of cowboy songs. In 1932, John Lomax was commissioned to compile a book of folk songs. Alan accompanied him, and they covered 16,000 miles of the U.S. in four months.

They would seek out songs in all sorts of places, including prisons, and record unknown musicians using a crude recording machine provided by the Library of Congress.

Cameron: Is it true that they made some prisoners famous?

Professor: Actually, yes. And one such musician was a prisoner whose release they helped secure, and whom they hired as their driver. His name was Huddie Ledbetter, whom you might know as Lead Belly, the legendary folk and blues guitarist.

You may not have heard him performing his own songs, but you have definitely heard others singing them. In the last few decades, his songs have been covered by musicians like Ry Cooder, Johnny Cash, the Beach Boys, and the White Stripes, among many others.

The more you listen to his music and of other musicians that the Lomaxes recorded, the more you see what a huge contribution to music and musicology they made. Alan went on to record music all over the world, and, more importantly, to work to make the music commercially available. Do you have a question, Richard?

Richard: I think I heard a recording of Lead Belly on the piano. I was just wondering what other instruments he played.

Professor: It might be a little easier to ask which instruments he *didn't* play. Besides guitar and piano, he played mandolin, harmonica, violin, concertina . . .

Unit 7 Self-study

Emma: Hi, Lucy. Where are you going?

Lucy: Hi, Emma. I'm just going out to that new farmers' market that opened last month.

Emma: You are? I thought it was supposed to be really expensive compared to the grocery store.

Lucy: No. Somebody told me about this blog where someone did a comparison between the farmers' market and the local supermarket. She spent about a third less shopping at the farmers' market than she would have at the supermarket.

Emma: Really? I would have thought it would be the other way around. Some of the dairy produce at the farmers' markets is so much **nicer**. There's that dairy farm where they make the cheese like they used to before we had all this pre-packaged stuff that's tasteless.

Lucy: The yogurt the dairy farm makes is excellent too. And you feel as though it's **more ethical** when you buy direct from the producer, don't you?

Emma: Yeah, I know what you mean. I think the producers you buy from at farmers' markets are usually **more concerned** about the care of the animals and the environment.

Lucy: Well, especially the organic farmers. I think they are the ones who really make a difference. They're growing crops the way farmers did years ago. And the fruit and vegetables are picked **later**. That's got to be **better** for everybody. And of course, it's a lot **fresher**.

Emma: Well, they haven't traveled as far across the country as supermarket produce either, of course, so they're much **more nutritious**. So, what were the prices she mentioned? Do you remember?

Lucy: Not exactly. But I remember thinking the biggest savings were on things like strawberries, cherries, potatoes – all the fresh fruits and vegetables were a much **better deal** – cheaper and **better quality**.

For instance, the strawberries at the supermarket, which were flown in and not especially fresh, were about a dollar a pound more. It's not *that* much on a single item, but it all adds up.

Emma: Yeah. If you think you're saving around a dollar an item, and you need to buy 20 things . . . then you're 20 dollars better off.

Lucy: Right – 20 dollars which you can then take over to the plant stall or the natural cosmetics stall or that really neat crafts stall . . .

Emma: Hang on a sec, let me get my purse. I'm coming with you.

Unit 8 Self-study

Andrea: Wow, Pauline, I'm exhausted. Let's get a cup of coffee. What about that salesperson? Talk about a hard sell!

Pauline: No kidding, Andrea. She was so **pushy**! She more or less demanded I buy that coat! It's **a shame**, because I really did like it, but I couldn't wait to get out of there.

Andrea: I don't know why some salespeople are like that. I mean, I'm much more likely to buy something if I'm just left alone.

Pauline: Well, I think it's important for a salesperson to offer to help customers, maybe suggest items to a customer . . .

Andrea: Oh, I don't really like it when they suggest things. Don't you think people have different shopping styles?

Pauline: Oh, definitely. Take my husband for instance. I don't know how many times I've come back from looking for something in the grocery store and he's standing there with a bunch of weird stuff in the cart, looking very proud of himself. If I ask him why, for example, he has decided to buy a **dozen** jars of pickled herring, he just looks hurt and says, "Because it's cheap and we *never* have pickled herring."

Andrea: My sister is the one who drives *me* crazy. Every time she comes to town we have to go to every single thrift shop. She then insists I buy stuff because it's such **a bargain**. She always says, "You'd pay a fortune for this normally. Here it costs you less than ten dollars!" I don't even want the stuff!

Pauline: So what do you do?

Andrea: I buy it. Then, after she leaves, I take it back and **donate** it *back* to the thrift shop.

Pauline: So you actually lose money! The salesperson must think you're crazy. Have you ever worked as a salesperson?

Andrea: No, have you?

Pauline: Yeah, I did, for a semester. I worked at Williams', in the shoe department. We had some real **nightmare** customers. There was this one woman who . . .

Unit 9 Self-study

Phil: This afternoon on *Job Talk* we have Fay Summer with us to tell us about an unusual occupation – pet psychology. Welcome to the show, Fay.

Fay: Thanks, Phil.

Phil: So you're one of the new Dr. Doolittles – someone who can talk to the animals! A pet psychologist.

Fay: No, not exactly, Phil. We prefer to refer to ourselves as applied animal behaviorists, not pet psychologists. Many of us, in fact, don't work with pets, which we call companion animals. Animal behaviorists may also work with farm animals – herds of cows, for example, zoo or laboratory animals, or, of course, with wild animals.

Phil: I see. So, the animals don't actually lie on a couch and tell you about their dreams – right?

Fay: Yes, you could put it that way. But I don't think you realize that these are qualified people doing a professional job – not just whatever they want to, whenever they think they can get away with it!

Phil: Ah, OK. I'm sorry if I sounded flippant. It's just that whenever I hear the words *pet* and *psychologist* in the same sentence, it does conjure up a certain stereotype – someone who's got some kind of an angle – and is charging a lot of money for it. But I guess, um, animal behaviorists are not just nutty animal lovers.

Fay: You're right. Most of us probably are animal lovers, and there are definitely a few nutty ones among us, but the qualifications *are* pretty demanding.

Phil: So, Fay, tell us, what is the usual pathway for becoming an animal behaviorist?

Fay: Animal behaviorists come from a variety of disciplines, including animal science, biology, psychology, or zoology. There are two levels of certification: Associate or Certified Applied Animal Behaviorist. Applicants have to have the right education, experience, and references.

So typically an Associate will have a master's degree in biology or behavioral science, and two years' experience in animal behavior; a Certified would typically have a doctorate and five years' experience.

Phil: I see. And what are the job prospects?

Fay: They're excellent. Wherever there are animals interacting with humans, there's a job.

Unit 10 Self-study

Professor: Good morning, everybody. Today we're going to be talking about ELF, English as a Lingua Franca. First off, can anyone tell me what the definition of a *lingua franca* is? Clea?

Clea: It's basically a common language used between groups that speak different languages to conduct business, commerce, isn't it?

Professor: Well, yes, business, commerce – life.

English is used as a lingua franca in many different areas of activity. About 85 percent of academic articles are in English. English is used in international business and finance, political negotiation, and tourism.

But most of this English is not so-called native-speaker English. The number of people who speak English is probably between about two and three billion. However, the majority of these people do not speak English as a first language. In the past, they were known as nonnative English speakers, but many people now feel that this classification is not particularly helpful. They would prefer to use the term *ELF speaker*, and some would also include speakers whose first language is English.

Now, many people are calling for a dictionary and a grammar of English as a Lingua Franca. But this is difficult for a number of reasons. Can anyone think of one?

Student: Well, is English as a Lingua Franca really grammatical? I mean, is it always grammatically correct?

Professor: Well, now that depends on what we mean by *grammatical*. The trend in English language teaching for about the last 40 years or so has been toward *describing* grammar that people use rather than *prescribing* grammar that they *should* use – in other words, explaining *how* people talk rather than telling them how they *should* talk.

So that's kind of a gray area. But, if we think of ELF as an evolving language variety, one that is not yet a clearly defined, standard variety like British Standard English or American Standard English, well, that might be more useful. Regardless, effective communication . . .

Unit 11 Self-study

Announcer: Welcome to *Be Your Best* with your host May Chan.

May: Today we're going to talk about life coaching. To tell us more about what life coaching actually is, we have Yolanda Peters, a widely respected life coach, with us in the studio today.

Welcome, Yolanda. Now, isn't life coaching really just a newly invented name for counseling or therapy?

Yolanda: Well, *some* people think that life coaching *is* just a new term for counseling. And, on the surface, that may appear to be so. But, in fact, that is not the case.

Of course, there are many different types of counseling, and different approaches to life coaching, but there is a key difference: Life coaching is more directive. A counselor will listen and occasionally comment, whereas a life coach is more action-oriented.

May: Well, haven't people been surviving all this time *without* a life coach? Do we really need people to tell us what to do?

Yolanda: Well, think about it like this: Everybody needs somebody who believes in them. Now, a life coach not only believes in you, but can also help you set goals and encourage you to achieve them and live the life you want to live.

It's not that different from a sports coach. In the same way he or she can help you improve your technique, a life coach can look at the big picture and advise you on how to make an effective, far-reaching plan to achieve your potential.

May: So what you're saying is that we tend to limit ourselves, and life coaches are in a position to see where those self-imposed limitations or problem areas are.

Yolanda: That's right. And, most importantly, how to solve them or work with them. Even the most deeply engrained habits can be broken or changed to work *for*, rather than against, a person's goals.

May: Do you think it's important for everyone to have clear goals?

Yolanda: Well, I think well-developed, achievable goals help give us a sense of accomplishment, which in turn makes us feel good about ourselves . . .

Unit 12 Self-study

Harry: Hi, Matt, what are you looking at?

Matt: Hi, Harry. It's a website about taking a year off. It's really interesting.

Harry: Career Man is thinking about taking a year off?

Matt: Maybe. Maybe not a whole year. Maybe a few months. I'm not sure.

Harry: What **brought** this **on**?

Matt: Well, it's just that over the holidays I was talking to my dad about his career and some of the choices he's made and, well, it was a bit of an eye-opener.

Harry: How so?

Matt: Dad said that if he'd had the chance, he would have lived abroad. Apparently he really wanted to go to Africa and work in a hospital there before we were born, but it didn't **work out**. He thinks that, if he had gone, he'd be a better doctor now.

Harry: Really?

Matt: Yeah, he felt really strongly about it. It made me think. Then when I **looked into** it, it's a lot easier nowadays.

Harry: So what would you like to do?

Matt: Provided I could find the right program, I think I'd like to get involved in a wildlife conservation project. There are a lot on this site – look.

Harry: Wow, I see what you mean. Habitat conservation, marine conservation, animal conservation – can you click on that one? Wow, working in an elephant sanctuary in Tanzania – how cool is that?

Matt: I know. You don't get paid, but what an experience! And it says here that, supposing you get accepted, you work alongside game wardens, vets, guides, and scientists.

Harry: Yeah, it doesn't really matter whether or not you get paid – you still **get** a lot **out of** it.

Matt: I like this one – marine conservation on a coral reef in the Philippines. I would just love that. And the thing is, provided you're working in an area related to what you eventually want to do as a career, employers are bound to be more interested in you if you have real experience.

Harry: I bet experience working in a program like that is going to look great on a résumé, whether it's in your area or not. I mean, it's got to show you're adaptable, adventurous . . .

Matt: Slightly nuts . . . I think you're getting into this idea.

Harry: I am!

Matt: Yeah, if this had existed 30 years ago, Dad would have been on a plane . . . Hey, look at this – "Community projects . . . ages 18 to 81" . . . I'm going to call Dad.

Self-study answer key

Unit 1 Self-study

Exercise 1

A

b. the first class reunion after ten years

B

a. 4   c. 1   e. 5

b. 3   d. 2

C

a. He thinks they're embarassing but funny.

Exercise 2

1. turn up   4. break down   7. show up
2. whip up   5. set up
3. track down   6. run through

Unit 2 Self-study

Exercise 1

A

c. good grooming

B

1. E   3. N   5. D   7. E

2. E   4. N   6. D   8. D

C

a. He is expressing an opinion.

Exercise 2

A

1. noun
2. 2 (noun and verb)
3. No.

B

2. noun, verb
3. noun, verb
4. adjective
5. noun, verb

Unit 3 Self-study

Exercise 1

A

c. information overload

B

1. True   3. False   5. True

2. True   4. False

C

c. very affected

Exercise 2

A

1. with
2. to
3. under

B

1. of   3. of   5. for   7. on

2. for, with   4. of   6. by   8. in

Unit 4 Self-study

Exercise 1

A

b. being a cartoonist

B

a. He collected cars.

e. He was a radio broadcaster, then had a TV show.

C

b. He has heard some negative things about Ripley.

Exercise 2

A

1. a   2. d   3. c   4. b

B

1. f   3. c   5. a
2. d   4. e   6. b

Unit 5 Self-study

Exercise 1

A

c. science and nature programs

B

1. True
2. False
3. True
4. False
5. False

C

b. They are very affected by the animals they film.

Exercise 2

A

1. a   3. d   5. b
2. c   4. e

B

1. surprisingly
2. unquestionably
3. obviously
4. presumably
5. instinctively
6. actually

Unit 6 Self-study

Exercise 1

A

c. folk and blues

B

a. 3   c. 4   e. 5
b. 2   d. 1

C

c. Lead Belly played a lot of instruments.

Exercise 2

A

1. humans, culture, society
2. living things
3. medical conditions of the heart
4. rocks
5. birds
6. words

B

1. **achievement**, **achiever**, achieve, achievable, –
2. **collection**, collector, collect, collectible, –
3. commerce, –, commercialize, commercial, **commercially**
4. music, **musician**, –, **musical**, musically
5. performance, performer, **perform**, –, –

Unit 7 Self-study

Exercise 1

A

c. The food is generally cheaper.

B

c, f, g, l, j, k

C

b. All of the strawberries at the supermarket were flown in and not very fresh.

Exercise 2

A

a. more nutritious
b. more ethical
c. more concerned

B

1. Noun = <u>con</u>tract; Verb = con<u>tract</u>
2. Noun = <u>pro</u>duce; Verb = pro<u>duce</u>
3. Noun = <u>rec</u>ord; Verb = re<u>cord</u>
4. Noun = re<u>lease</u>; Verb = release
5. Noun = <u>won</u>der; Verb = <u>won</u>der

Unit 8 Self-study

Exercise 1

A

c. The salesperson was too forceful.

B

1. True
2. True
3. False
4. False
5. True

C

a. herself

Exercise 2

A

1. dozen
2. a shame
3. nightmare
4. bargain
5. donate
6. pushy

B

1. alone
3. bunch
4. cart
5. stuff
6. fortune
7. leaves

C

b. She's annoyed because Phil doesn't seem to take the profession seriously.

Exercise 2

Flock: birds, goats, sheep
Herd: cows, elephants
School: fish

Unit 9 Self-study

Exercise 1

A

1. Associate
2. Certified

B

1. b, d, e, f
2. b, c, g, h

Unit 10 Self-study

Exercise 1

A

c. an evolving variety or varieties of English

B

1. True
2. True
3. False
4. False

C

a. The professor thinks the definition is too narrow.

Exercise 2

A

g. suggest strongly

B

1. f   3. e
2. b   4. c

Unit 11 Self-study

Exercise 1

A

b. Life coaching is more directive.

B

a, b

C

c. She thinks life coaching and counseling or therapy are the same.

Exercise 2

A

c. to seem

B

2. g   4. e   6. h   8. a
3. i   5. f   7. b   9. c

Unit 12 Self-study

Exercise 1

A

b. taking a year off

B

1. False   3. True   5. False
2. True   4. False

C

c. He thinks it's a surprising choice for Matt.

Exercise 2

A

1. a
2. c
3. d
4. b

B

1. got, out of
2. brought, on
3. look into
4. work out

Acknowledgments

Illustration credits

Charlene Chua: 3, 12, 28, 29, 53, 56
Peter Hoey: 10, 31, 69, 72, 87, 103
Kim Johnson: 65, 84, 101

Peter McDonnell: 38, 86
Sandy Nichols: 22, 23, 26, 40, 64, 76, 77

Photography credits

2 ©Inmagine. **5** ©Inmagine. **6** (*left to right*) ©Inmagine; ©Rolf Bruderer/Corbis; ©Inmagine. **8** ©Inmagine. **9** ©Kain Zernitsky/Getty Images. **11** ©Kjeld Duits/Japanese Streets. **13** ©Paul Doyle/Alamy. **14** ©Inmagine. **15** ©Inmagine. **16** (*clockwise from top right*) ©Tony Barson/Getty Images; ©Michael Tullberg/Getty Images; ©Fotos International/Getty Images; ©Scott Gries/Getty Images. **17** ©Inmagine. **18** (*left to right*) ©istockphoto; ©Javier Pierini/Getty Images; ©istockphoto. **19** ©istockphoto. **20** ©Shutterstock. **21** ©dreamstime. **24** ©Inmagine. **25** ©Dennis MacDonald/PhotoEdit. **27** (*clockwise from top left*) ©Andrew Paterson/Alamy; ©Car Culture/Getty Images; ©Photo Researchers, Inc.; ©Inga Spence/Getty Images; ©Moritz Steiger/Getty Images; ©istockphoto. **32** (*clockwise from top left*) ©Inmagine; ©Juniors Bildarchiv/Alamy; ©Michael Freeman/Corbis; ©West Country Farmhouse Cheesemakers Ltd/cheddarvision.tv. **33** ©istockphoto. **34** ©Gerard Cerles/Getty Images. **35** ©Jack Novak/Superstock. **37** ©Screenscope, Inc. **39** ©CBS Photo Archive/Getty Images. **42** ©Inmagine. **44** ©Inmagine. **45** ©Inmagine. **46** (*left to right*) ©Inmagine; ©Kevin Foy/Alamy; ©Inmagine. **47** (*left to right*) ©Michael Ochs Archives/Corbis; ©Michael Ochs Archives/Getty Images. **48** (*left to right*) ©Tim Mosenfelder/Getty Images; ©Vince Bucci/Getty Images; ©Bryan Bedder/DCP/Getty Images. **49** ©Jaume Gual/Age Fotostock. **50** ©Inmagine. **51** ©Dennis Kitchen. **52** ©Mika/Everitt Collection. **54** ©Inmagine. **57** ©Inmagine. **58** (*left to right*) ©Hamish and Fin Moore; ©Inmagine; ©Hara Kiyoshi. **59** ©Buzz Pictures/Alamy. **62** (*clockwise from top left*) ©Inmagine; ©Inmagine; ©Inmagine; ©Inmagine. **63** ©Inmagine. **66** (*left to right*) ©Vincent MacNamara/Alamy; ©Bill Aron/PhotoEdit; ©Bill Aron/PhotoEdit. **67** ©Nico Kai/Getty Images. **70** (*clockwise from top left*) ©Michel Boutefeu/Getty Images; ©Jon Freeman/Getty Images; ©N'Kisi Partnership, 2001/Grace Roselli; ©Jeffrey L. Rotman/Corbis. **71** ©Chung Sung-Jun/Getty Images. **73** ©Jeff Topping/Getty Images. **74** © Shutterstock. **75** ©Inmagine. **78** (*left to right*) ©Inmagine; ©Inmagine; ©Inmagine. **79** (*left to right*) ©Pete Oxford/Getty Images; ©Jeff Hunter/Getty Images; ©Inmagine. **80** (*left to right*) ©Lebrecht Music and Arts Photo Library/Alamy; ©Interfoto/Alamy. **82** ©Inmagine. **83** ©Inmagine. **85** ©Inmagine. **88** (*left to right*) ©Hulton-Deutsch Collection/Corbis; ©Lorenzo Santini/Getty Images; ©Alexander Hassenstein/Getty Images. **90** (*clockwise from top left*) ©Hulton Archive/Getty Images; ©Keystone/Getty Images; ©Interfoto/Alamy; ©Howard Sochurek/Getty Images; ©Carl Mydans/Getty Images. **91** ©Eamonn McCormack/Getty Images. **92** (*top to bottom*) ©istockphoto; ©istockphoto; ©Inmagine; ©Inmagine; ©istockphoto; ©Inmagine. **93** ©Inmagine. **94** ©Inmagine. **95** ©CAMFED. **96** (*clockwise from top left*) ©Boris Roessler/Corbis; ©Richard Smith/Corbis; ©Stuart Isett. **100** ©Erik Dreyer/Getty Images. **102** ©Inmagine. **105** (*left to right*) ©Stephen Oliver/Alamy; ©Inmagine; ©Inmagine.

Text credits

The authors and publishers are grateful for permission to reprint the following items:

9 Adapted from "The Value of Cyber-Friendship" by Jason Lee Miller, www.webpronews.com, January 26, 2006. Copyright © 2006. Reprinted with permission from WebProNews. **16** Adapted from "Judging Faces Comes Naturally" by Jules Crittenden, *Boston Herald*, September 7, 1997, page 10. Reprinted with permission of the *Boston Herald*. **17** Adapted from "First Impressions Count; Appearance Must Match Personality" by Eva Neumann, www.monstersandcritics.com, December 28, 2006. **25** Adapted from "Who Are the Amish?" BBC News, October 2, 2006. Reprinted with permission from BBC News at www.bbc.co.uk/news. **35** Adapted from "The Infamous Hope Diamond" by G. L. Byez. Reprinted with permission of G. L. Byez, www.finejewelrydesigns.com. **51** Adapted from "Striving to Make Music Under the Streets of NYC" by Daniel Strieff and Jon Sweeney, *MSNBC*, August 26, 2004. Copyright © 2004. MSNBC Interactive News, LLC. Reprinted with permission. **61** Adapted from "More People Are Leaving the Rat Race for the Simple Life" by Julia Duin, *The Washington Times*, January 22, 1996, page 23. Copyright © 1996 News World Communications, Inc. Reprinted with permission from *The Washington Times*. **69** Adapted from "The Rise of 'Guerilla' Marketing" by Bill Emmott, *The Economist*, October 12, 2000. Copyright © 2000. Economist Newspaper Group. Reprinted with permission. **77** Adapted from "Kennel of the Mind" by Drew Hinshaw, *Metro New York*, July 16, 2007. Reprinted with permission of Drew Hinshaw. **80** Adapted from *Schaum's Quick Guide to Great Presentation Skills* by Melody Templeton and Suzanne Sparks Fitzgerald. Copyright © 1999 by the McGraw-Hill Companies, Inc., page 16. **87** Adapted from "Slang Abroad" by Ben Falk, *The Daily Colonial*, April 1, 2006. **95** Adapted from "Leading Questions: An Interview with Ann Cotton, Social Entrepreneur" interview by Alison Benjamin, *The Guardian*, March 28, 2007. Copyright © Guardian News & Media Ltd 2007. **103** From the book titled *Job Savvy: How to Be a Success at Work*, by LaVerne L. Ludden, Ed.D., Copyright © 2008, JIST Publishing, Indianapolis, Indiana. Used with permission of the publisher. To order, contact JIST Publishing at 1-800-648-5478.

Every effort has been made to trace the owners of copyrighted material in this book. We would be grateful to hear from anyone who recognizes his or her copyrighted material and who is unacknowledged. We will be pleased to make the necessary corrections in future editions of the book.

Answers

Page 32, Exercise 1B: Story 2 is false.
Page 34, Exercise 5B: They are all hoaxes.

Page 84, Exercise 2A: before, are you OK, See you later, excellent, great, tonight